Acclaim for *The Enlightenment of Work*

'A far-reaching and inspiring look at the world of work and why we often feel trapped in the work we do. This is a must-read for anyone looking to have a happier, more authentic career experience that brings bliss and flow into everyday work. I found a number of indispensable, practical ideas here that have transformed my view of the work I do and why I do it. Highly recommended.'
—**Tania Ahsan**, Editor of *Kindred Spirit*

'Steve Nobel has beautifully blended ancient Buddhist wisdom with modern insights, reflections, stories and practical exercises that offer to help transform your current work experience from necessity to opportunity and possibility. Instead of suffering you can grow and learn from the inside out.'
—**Shamash Alidina**, author of *Mindfulness for Dummies*

'A thought-provoking entree into how our evolving perceptions and attitudes mould our lives. An indispensable reference guide as to how to live a more fulfilling life in both your personal and working environment.'
—**Hazel Courteney**, author, broadcaster and journalist

'Steve Nobel elegantly shows us how to transform the samsara of meaningless work to the bliss of fulfilling work that is aligned with our soul's true destiny. A vital message of "awakened action" for today's world.'
—**Amoda Maa Jeevan**, author of *Change your Life, Change your World*

'An inspiring, powerful meditation on work, relevant to anyone whether happy at work or not.'
—**Nina Grunfeld**, author of *The Life Book* and founder of Life Clubs

'Steve Nobel walks his talk. He knows from personal experience what it means to be unhappy at work, and he has found solutions that uplift, enrich and lead to greater fulfilment. A must read!'
—**Ed and Deb Shapiro**, authors of *Be The Change: How Meditation Can Transform You and the World*

'It's not often a book manages to be so inspirational and informative, compassionate and practical, clear and thorough, simple and deep. This is the spiritual and compassionate path to finding your right work and loving what you do. Steve Nobel's approach to the world of work is inspired, insightful, practical, very real and truthful. A must read!'
—**Arielle Essex**, author of *Compassionate Coaching* and NLP Trainer

'This book is a breath of fresh air for anyone who wants to find a way to create more meaningful work. I love the blend of both modern and ancient teachings that gives work spirit and soul.'
—**Jackee Holder**, author of *Soul Purpose* and *Be Your Own Best Life Coach*

the
enlightenment
of
WORK

Revealing the Path
to Happiness, Contentment
and Purpose in Your Job

STEVE NOBEL

WATKINS PUBLISHING
LONDON

This edition first published in the UK and USA 2012 by
Watkins Publishing, Sixth Floor, Castle House,
75–76 Wells Street, London W1T 3QH

Design and typography copyright © Watkins Publishing 2012
Text Copyright © Steve A Nobel 2012

1 3 5 7 9 10 8 6 4 2

Designed and typeset by Jerry Goldie Graphic Design

Printed and bound in China by Imago

British Library Cataloguing-in-Publication Data Available

Library of Congress Cataloging-in-Publication Data Available

ISBN: 978-1-78028-381-4

www.watkinspublishing.co.uk

Distributed in the USA and Canada by Sterling Publishing Co., Inc.
387 Park Avenue South, New York, NY 10016-8810

For information about custom editions, special sales, premium and
corporate purchases, please contact Sterling Special Sales
Department at 800-805-5489 or specialsales@sterlingpub.com

Contents

Dedication

This book is dedicated to you and your descendants – may you courageously step onto the path that leads to seek a more enlightened way at work.

Acknowledgements

I would like to thank all the authors, teachers, guides and mentors whose insight and wisdom have touched and transformed me. In particular, I would like to give thanks to Laurence Boldt, Michael Breen, Joseph Campbell, Gill Edwards, Matthew Fox, Thich Nhat Hanh, Lama Surya Das, David Whyte and Nick Williams for the work and inspiration they have generously shared with the world.

A big thank you to all my friends and colleagues at the fabulous Alternatives, based at St James's Church. The love and generosity of the staff and volunteers there seem boundless!

Thank you to all the authors, coaches, teachers and friends who have taken the time to review and endorse this work.

Lastly I want to thank my children, Peter and Lynda, and my grand-daughters Eva and Isabella. I am their silent and often their not-so-silent cheerleader.

Last but not least, I want to thank the being known as the Buddha who incarnated some 2,500 years ago on the borders of Nepal and India. His radiant consciousness, wisdom, teaching and example have helped turn countless numbers to the light.

Introduction

This may seem an obvious statement, but here goes, anyway – many people around the world are now suffering in their work in some way. Not everyone suffers, but many do: millions, perhaps even billions. I know about suffering at work from personal experience. I suffered for many years. I have done my time!

And so here is my message to you about suffering. First, suffering can come in many ways. It can come through feeling aimless and bored when the only reason for being at work is to collect the pay cheque at the end of the month. It can come through stress, overwork and burnout. Sometimes, it comes through overarching ambition, when we have tried too hard and for too long to climb up the corporate ladder, only to find it is leaning in the wrong direction. There are always challenges at work and there will always be the inevitable disappointment and frustration. Sometimes, suffering arises through unrealistic expectations, when we are not able to see the truth in a situation.

Wherever there are relationships there can be disagreement. Sometimes disagreement can be creative, sometimes not. When it is not it can lead to manipulation, conflict and even bullying. We can suffer when we are without work for short or long periods.

Whatever our work, there is always the possibility that we can feel exposed to being undervalued, criticized or harshly judged. Suffering can come through feeling trapped in a job that feels joyless or hard – we may feel we have little say in the content or context of our work. We may feel unable to follow a direction that gives a sense of meaning or joy. We may feel that we are incapable of making the kinds of changes to our work we would most like.

Suffering can be physical, emotional, mental and even spiritual. There is the kind of physical suffering that arises when the stress or joylessness of work creates ongoing tension in the body. This, is turn, can lead to ill-health and serious illness. There are degrees of emotional suffering when we feel anger, grief, misery and unhappiness at work. We can suffer mentally by recycling thoughts around failure, insignificance and powerlessness – these thoughts can coalesce into fixed beliefs that say we cannot positively influence or shape our destiny in any way. Then there is spiritual suffering which is more commonplace than you may think. This arises when our work disconnects us from our true essence.

Whatever the cause of suffering, it can easily start in one area and then spread. Physical suffering will tend to lead to emotional, mental and, sometimes, spiritual suffering. For instance, if you have a physical injury that prevents you from doing certain activities, then it can be hard not to have certain thoughts and feelings about this. Suffering can be infectious. If you are long-term unemployed, then your stress can so easily touch those you come into daily contact with. In our celebrity culture where the bright and the beautiful are seen as good, suffering is seen as something bad; something to be shunned and kept at a distance. We read about suffering in the newspapers and that is as close as it should get. Suffering is seen as an illness, as shameful, as something that must be avoided at all costs. When it comes knocking at our door, we feel that we should hide away and not speak of it. 'Keep a stiff upper lip,' and all of that.

There is a difference between pain and suffering. Pain cannot be avoided. Pain is something we will all encounter at some point. We may be the most optimistic, affirming person on the planet, yet we will still encounter pain. We cannot keep it at bay forever. Hopefully, when pain comes we will know how to use it to uplift us and allow ourselves to grow and move on.

Suffering can be avoided. When we deny pain, then we create unnecessary suffering. When we suppress the pain of certain feelings, then we create suffering that may take any number of forms. This is like trying to force shut the lid on a boiling saucepan – not a good idea.

The good news is that we can unravel patterns of suffering. The good news is that just as suffering happens, so too can inspiration, joy, love and possibility. Life can be an amazingly rich tapestry of experience and growth. This book has a simple philosophy: suffering happens; there is no merit in suffering; suffering can be embraced and transformed; when we truly transform suffering, then something different can be experienced.

I suffered considerably for the first ten years of my working life from a deep sense of meaninglessness and depression. I could see no point in the work I was doing. I had no real affinity with it. Worse than that, I deeply questioned the ethics of some of the things I was working on. For instance, for some years my day would start with processing paperwork dealing with the export of arms to various foreign regimes. Not the most inspiring work I have done in my life!

There were other aspects of my work that I was not sure about, such as offering huge loans to finance what seemed to me to be rather grand projects in many developing countries. Such loans kept these countries tied to high interest payments and debt for many years. I had very little say over my day-to-day work, it was initiated elsewhere and some of it landed on my desk for processing. It did not matter a hoot whether I agreed with it or not; I was there to toe the company line, and I was not in a position to argue the matter. I looked to see if anyone else shared my feelings of disquiet and unease, but the vast majority seemed quite happy to get on with it. As long as they got paid every month and could drown their sorrows with a few beers, all was well. But for me all was not well – I felt deeply unhappy and unfulfilled.

As long as I remember working in that job I had strong migraines that would just emerge unexpectedly. There were an assortment of other minor ailments – nothing serious, but it went on for many years. I sought relief through changing my diet, macrobiotics, yoga, tai chi, and different forms of meditation. I discovered eventually that the source of my suffering was nothing to do with my lifestyle – it was everything to do with what I was doing. In time, the build-up of tension and stress led me to take time out – around a year, in fact. The physical tension subsided, but the depression stayed. My ten years in banking were at an end, but where next? I could not see a particularly bright future.

During this period of convalescence, and with the support of a psycho-therapy group, I began to unearth much that was previously unexamined in myself. I found a new job in an inner city borough in the Housing Directorate, working with special needs and elderly tenants. I had moved from a structured, conservative environment to a socialist, idealistic and rather chaotic environment. This was not without its challenges, but I felt more at home and discovered abilities I did not know I had. I discovered that I was good with people, that I was able to manage and problem solve. I started to trust myself and develop my intuition.

My depression eventually faded and in its place emerged a latent passion for spirituality. I began to attend spiritual and personal development workshops which helped me transform different aspects of my life, but my work still felt out of sync with my heart and spirit. I was promoted to a good position, but this did not really help much. I was feeling the winds of change calling once more. My heart was telling me that now was the time to leave, but my head said stay. Since I was more spiritually aware, I decided to ask my innermost spirit, Higher Self, the Universe (the name felt unimportant) a question: 'Should I resign from this job?' I waited, and within 48 hours I received the answer. During a lunch break as I was walking back to work one day there was a guy walking in front of me several feet ahead. On the back of his T-shirt there was the Nike slogan saying, 'Just do it'. The message hit me like a thunderbolt, but my mind cut across, very quickly discounting the message. I was reminded by a stream of thoughts that I had responsibili-ties and should not throw everything away because of some random slogan on a T-shirt. As I continued walking, my attention was drawn to a nearby window and there was a sticker with the same message: 'Just do it'. Okay, that was it – I gave in, I surrendered, and very soon after handed in my letter of resignation.

I can still remember the bliss of that day and how grey everyone else in the workplace seemed. Thus began my next adventure with work. Now I had let go of the 'safe' career and, instead, I threw myself into every kind of job that I could find. I painted houses, I did landscape gardening, I sold books, I sold health products, I worked in an office, I made tea. I was noticing when I was in flow and when I was struggling. I learnt that chasing jobs put me in struggle. The more I trusted the process, the more I felt in flow.

During this time I started doing some part-time work for an amazing organization called Alternatives, based in St James's Church, Piccadilly, London. After a year or so, they offered me the job of full-time administrator. I was not so keen on doing administration, but I loved the organization, so I accepted. I continued doing personal development seminars and discovered interesting concepts such as values and untapped gifts. After a year of admin I was offered a directorship of Alternatives. Within a short period of time two other co-directors resigned and I found that I was running the organization alone. Not having much business experience, I meditated and prayed. Fortunately, the Universe was listening and responded. I was guided to employ the perfect people for the right jobs and take some important decisions to restore the organization to a place of high morale and financial stability and abundance.

As I write this, I have been a director of Alternatives for just over ten years. Here I learnt to play and to be creative. I learnt more about the power of generosity and 'what goes around comes around'. I learnt about the importance of community and of finding 'the right tribe'. In 2001 I started to write my first book and now I am a published author: this is my third book.

Writing is something I have come to love dearly – both the research aspect and the creative aspect. Around 2004 I began to get interested in coaching and NLP, and after a few years of training I started a personal and business coaching company which I now run part time. Also, I have been running retreats and workshops for several years now. More recently, I started a podcasting section on my website, where I interview different authors and teachers in spiritual awakening, personal development, coaching, business and work and make them available as free resources. All of the above continue to be a great source of inspiration and joy for me.

This book has been a journey of tremendous discovery for me – researching and writing it has changed my views on work and growth. And this is as it should be – as the Buddha says, nothing is permanent. This book draws on wisdom from a number of sources, primarily Buddhism, Coaching/NLP and Taoism. Although I have presented many stories, ideas and meditations that are Buddhist, this is not a book about being a Buddhist. You do not have to believe in anything that is written herein. I simply encourage you to try on some of the ideas for size and see what happens. I offer this book in the spirit of adventure, compassion and service, in the hope that it will help you find your own unique way to transform suffering and navigate to the limitless possibilities beyond.

You can use this book to transform your own limiting attitudes and perspectives regarding the work you do, and open yourself to new ways of behaving. This will certainly allow more peace, joy and possibility to arise within your existing work. You can also use this book to explore changing your work itself. Changing your attitudes and perspectives on what is possible for you will certainly help. Learning to be more authentic, resourceful, intuitive, playfully creative and in the flow will also help you. You may not know what you want as an end result, so use this book as an aid to your process of gaining more clarity. Let the ideas and methodologies of this book lead you in the direction of your heart – towards the boundless experience of peace, purpose, passion, enthusiasm, giftedness, flow, wisdom, joy and bliss in your work.

Steve Ahnael Nobel, 2011

Chapter 1

Why Suffer?

All the world is full of suffering.
It is also full of overcoming.

Helen Keller

· ·

Prince Siddhartha was born in 563 BC in Nepal near the Himalayas to a rich and royal family. Just before his birth, his mother had a dream that a white elephant entered her womb through her side. A wise man interpreted this dream, saying that the child would either be a world leader or a monk. His mother died two days after giving birth and so the young prince was raised by his father in a palace beneath the majestic mountains of the Himalayas. The King, determined that his son would not be a monk, gave orders that he should never leave the palace grounds. At the age of 16, his father arranged his marriage to a beautiful princess. To keep him further distracted, he built a richly ornate palace for the couple. Here, only young, beautiful and healthy people were allowed. But the prince became restless and wanted to venture beyond the palace grounds.

Eventually, he found a way to leave for short periods. On his first visit to a nearby town he encountered old age. On his second visit he came across sickness. And on his third visit he witnessed death – yet he also met a holy man who appeared content and at peace with the world. The prince felt so moved by the sight of the monk that he abandoned royal life and took up the spiritual quest. For the next six years he explored ascetic life, and experienced prolonged fasting and exposure to hardship and pain. Exhausted, he accepted some rice-milk from a young woman and henceforth decided to follow the path of moderation between the extremes of self-indulgence and self-denial. He sat in meditation under a fig tree, henceforth known as 'The Tree of Awakening', and vowed not to arise again until he had achieved enlightenment. After many days of meditation he was able to see deeply into the nature of suffering and, finally, he awakened as 'The Buddha', also known as the 'Enlightened One'.

Work and Suffering ...

Unlike the early life of Prince Siddhartha, most of us are destined to perform some work in the world. Work can happen in the home or out in the world. Work can be a rich source of joy or a source of suffering. Many people are suffering in their work unnecessarily. In some developing countries, where workers receive poor pay in return for long, hard hours, work is no better than slave labour. Often, these same workers feel trapped because they have no voice, no freedom to organize, and they feel generally exploited.

In the developed West, work can also be a source of suffering, where human dignity is squashed by overwork, stress, criticism, bullying, and uncaring employment practices. Many feel unhappy in their work, and many feel unhappy that they have no work. The scale of the problem is huge.

Work was not always such a source of misery. Before the Industrial Revolution in Britain, people worked close to the land and in communities. It is a myth that people worked in dreary conditions from dawn to dusk. Before the Industrial Revolution, according to some accounts, the tempo of life was relatively slow and leisurely and the pace of work was quite relaxed. The pre-Industrial calendar was filled with holidays – mostly religious – and there was also plenty of time for feasting and merrymaking. This all changed, of course, as factories and mills and railroads began to dominate the landscape. Coupled with religious ideas on the righteousness of the work ethic, work quickly turned into an activity that was long, hard and stressful, where time was something not to be enjoyed, but exchanged for money.

Over the past few centuries, we have been conditioned with some unhealthy ideas that need to be undone if we are going to transform our rather unhappy way of thinking about work in the Western world. Viktor Frankl was a survivor of a Nazi concentration camp and he wrote about his experience and insights just after the war in his book *Man's Search for Meaning*. Frankl wrote about three psychological reactions experienced by concentration camp inmates: the first was shock when people were admitted to the camp; the second was apathy as inmates became accustomed to camp existence; and the third was depersonalization and disillusionment. Does any of this sound familiar? It is bizarre to note that the sign welcoming the millions of unfortunate inmates into many concentration camps, including Auschwitz and Dachau, read 'Work makes you free'.

An Absence of Work

The effects of unemployment can range from emotional trauma to problems with being hired in the future. Being made redundant or being fired may mean a change of career. If you had planned a certain career path with a particular level of advancement and incremental salary, then this may cause you to suffer. Being unemployed can generate feelings of apathy, discouragement and embarrassment. Not working can lead to a crisis of meaning and a certain lack of connection and engagement with the world.

Losing a job for a short period of time can cause stress and even depression. Where unemployment is longer term the psychological problems of decreased self-esteem, stress and depression may be more far reaching. The stress of long-term unemployment will tend to impact friends and family also. In times of mass unemployment there can be a collective gloom that descends on a country. Various studies point to there being a statistical correlation between unemployment and crime, suicide and mental illness.

Meaningless Work

A major source of suffering arises when work feels dull and meaningless. There is an old English proverb that says, 'All work and no play makes Jack a dull boy.' The original meaning of the word dull was more akin to stupid than boring. Nowadays, there are many jobs that are simply dull. Some jobs are little more than paper shuffling – some jobs are about making senseless widgets – some jobs are highly repetitive.

What is not so well known is that dull work is a killer. According to a study conducted by University College London Medical School, some workers may actually do themselves a favour by not showing up for dull work. According to the report, 'Men with low-paying jobs and less education have a higher risk for heart disease, a trend that has been evident for the last 30 years.' When it comes to this kind of work it is sad to see someone going through the motions, just turning up, doing what needs to be done and then heading off home. There is no spark and no passion. Often the lights are on but there is no one at home!

Shallow Work

One of my favourite films is *Before Sunrise* which tells of a love story between two young people meeting for the first time on a train to Paris. Jesse is a good-looking young American guy on his way back to the States and Celine a beautiful young French woman returning to her home in Paris after visiting her grandmother. Celine tells Jesse about her father who is always thinking of her future career. Celine would say to her father she wanted to be a writer and he would respond by saying, 'So you want to be a journalist?' Celine would say she wanted to be an actress and her father would say she should be a TV newscaster. Celine would say she wanted to create a refuge for stray cats and her father would reply with the career of veterinarian. Celine complained, 'It was this constant conversion of my fanciful ambition into these practical, money-making ventures.'

Chasing money can eventually become a source of suffering. Money, in itself, cannot provide real meaning. Yes, money is important to live in the modern world, to pay the bills and support a family, but work is about so much more than money. The question worth asking is, how much money can compensate you for a life unfulfilled?

Stressful Work

We can suffer at work through busyness, overwork and stress. Work is often challenging, presenting various deadlines, frustrations and demands. Work may require us to work long hours or even spend hours commuting. Stress in small doses can be a motivating force, but when stress is ongoing it can lead to feeling frazzled and overwhelmed. If it goes on for too long it will then feel like a way of life. The effects of stress increase or decrease in relation to a number of factors, such as strength or weakness in the following areas: our network of family and supportive friends; self-awareness and emotional intelligence; optimistic attitude; and level of self-confidence.

Stress can also be a killer – studies show that the stress of returning to work after the weekend can trigger a dangerous increase in blood pressure – leading to death from heart attacks and strokes which tend to peak on a Monday morning.

Driven Work

Ambition can lead to unhappiness. A good friend of mine studied to be a doctor and early on, her group was asked what motivated them to want to be doctors. One by one the students responded, and mostly the answers revolved around money and status. When it was her turn, she said she wanted a job that could really help people and make a positive contribution to their lives. She told me that there was an uncomfortable silence in the room after she answered. It was a rude awakening for her that most of the other students were not motivated in the same way that she was.

Ambition alone may not sustain you through a lifetime of work. Ambition is certainly a motivating force, but it is less reliable an ally than enthusiasm. The word 'enthusiasm' comes from the Greek language, meaning 'to be possessed by a God'. Ambition can lead us to climbing the executive ladder and getting a bigger mortgage, but ambition without enthusiasm can lead to suffering. I have met many people who create a series of goals for their lives that goes something like: 'By the age of 21 I will get a first-class honours degree in my chosen subject, then I will have an MA by the age of 22, then I will travel the world for a year, then I will get a top job in a company I have been researching,' and on it goes. If the drive and focus are strong, then these goals may well be reached. But having such a check list is no sure way to long-term happiness.

For some, the ambition is so strong that it tips into negative ambition. This is where an excessive desire for something leads to suffering early on. Perhaps the negative ambition manifests as greed and selfishness where the needs or rights of others are sacrificed by the burning desire to reach a goal.

Stuck Work

Feeling stuck or trapped in a line of work is a source of misery. You may feel stuck in a job and unable to move on because you feel you have been there too long; the pay is good; you have invested too much in it; you have bills to pay and moving is risky; you have a family to consider and so staying put seems the simplest option; you are too old to move, or you feel you lack the competencies and skills to move towards what you really want to do.

In some places the culture itself creates stuckness. For instance, in India, over 260 million women, children and men belong to the 'Untouchable' caste. The caste system in India determines people's social status, potential marriage partners, access to education, and work. Although the term untouchable was banned under the Indian constitution some 60 years ago, 'Untouchables' are still relegated to the lowest jobs in society. Their occupations are often the same as those of their parents.

Violent Work

Conflict is, unfortunately, a very common cause of misery at work. Whereas creative disagreement can lead to new ideas and possibilities, destructive conflict rarely produces anything useful. Whenever there are big egos on the loose in the workplace, conflict and disagreement are bound to happen. Also, whenever there are major changes on the horizon, this can lead to conflict. When people feel insecure and afraid, they may react defensively and aggressively.

Bullying at work is a very specific form of conflict. This can inflict suffering on others, especially when it is constant and spiteful. It is usually – though not always – done to someone in a 'lower' position. Bullying can come in different forms: face to face, by letter, through a phone call, by email, or through social media messaging. There are various ways people can feel harassed in the workplace, including feeling: constantly picked on or criticized; humiliated in front of colleagues; regularly treated unfairly; verbally abused; blamed for problems not of their making; or threatened with punishments. It is important to feel respected and safe in the workplace, otherwise this can lead to suffering.

Insecure Work

In the past there was the notion of a job for life and at the end of a long period of dedicated service you could then expect a pension and perhaps a gold watch and framed certificate. I still remember my grandfather's gold watch and the certificate hanging on his bedroom wall honouring his 40 years of service. I used to look at that certificate with great admiration and wonder about his work. At the time, I had no concept of how long 40 years really was.

Now it seems a really long time to stay in one place. Now there is no job for life and this can be a source of excitement and adventure or insecurity and clinging, depending on your point of view. When the fear of uncertainty is strong, there may be a fear of rocking the boat or taking risks. This can block the possibility of trying anything new. Where there is a lack of courage, or higher or broader vision, this can prevent you from fully embracing the possibilities of your life which, in turn, creates suffering.

Work: Beyond Suffering ...

The really sad thing in selling our time to a job that we are unhappy in is that we are selling a commodity that is finite. Our time on this earth will eventually run out and this is a resource we will never recover, at least not in this lifetime! On the other hand, the good news is that suffering at work is not mandatory, it is optional, and the person who decides whether you suffer or not is not the boss, the company, your government or your culture – it is you.

Some circumstances may feel very challenging, but it is not so much the circumstances but your reaction to the circumstances that is important. Victor Frankl said, 'Every human being has the ability to change at every instant.' There is a way out of suffering, and that way has to be chosen consciously. Suffering is a form of feedback that tells us something is amiss, that something needs to change. Nowadays in the Western world, we are being called to take charge of our destiny – our working lives are no longer largely organized for us, there is no job for life any more. The values of our parents and grandparents cannot guide us as they could in previous decades. As long as we are suffering we will never realize that there is anything else available.

THE FOUR POSSIBILITIES

1. There is the possibility that at some point in your work you will suffer, either physically, emotionally, mentally or even spiritually.

2. There is the possibility that you will transform your suffering and go beyond it to explore a new way, a more healthy and joyful way.

3. There is the possibility that you will know your true nature, become more resourceful, play instead of work hard, know your heartfelt values, follow your true direction, and find or create work that you love.

4. There is the possibility that you will learn to flow, take effortless action, open to grace and awaken to bliss in your work.

When we manage to go beyond suffering in our work, there are many new possibilities that can open up to us.

Work and Meaning

The world of work we are entering into demands that we are on track, have a sense of direction and purpose, and seek to make a meaningful contribution to others. Perhaps the job is a stepping stone to something greater. Perhaps the job is a way of getting clear about one's true direction in life. Purpose is an inner fire, a clarity, a heightened sense of aliveness. Purpose shines through the eyes, body language, the way a person speaks and moves through the world; there is a vibrancy in the voice. Purpose is about knowing where you are going and why you are going there. Purpose is like falling in love – you do not know what it is until you experience it for the first time. Purpose is visionary rather than goal driven. Here we become the artists of our working lives. No longer limited by the dreams and hopes of others, we let our own dreams soar and take flight.

Work and Presence

The world of work we are entering into demands that we are awake and conscious, rather than asleep or on autopilot. When work is painful we will avoid that pain with all manner of things that put us to sleep. When we are awake we are more present in what we do. When our work is a source of suffering we cannot be present in it. We can be simultaneously alert to danger and seek to be elsewhere in our minds.

When we enjoy what we are doing and enjoy the people we work with, then we will be more present. This can transform even the most menial kind of work. I have met people who do very menial tasks and bring to it such care, devotion and joy that they uplift everyone around them. I have seen joyful and attentive cleaners and met focused assembly-line workers, bubbly sales-people, and genuinely warm receptionists. I once knew a Jesuit priest who commanded great respect simply because of the power of his presence. He listened and spoke with great attention and focus. He never rushed, always taking his time, and gave very thoughtful responses. He brought a great presence to everything he did and everyone he met. Presence is one of the qualities that we can bring to enhance our experience of work.

Work and Courage

The world of work we are entering into demands that we be courageous. For centuries, we have been taught to conform to a system. The current working climate does not favour conformity, it favours courage. Courage is about maintaining a healthy individuality when working with others. It takes courage to know our values and to work by them. This can be challenging in some working environments, for sure. When things are tough, courage is the pivotal energy that can flip us out of situations our head says we must endure. Without courage, we will simply endure situations that we should not! Courage makes us stand up and speak out. Courage makes us move when we need to move. Courage leads to tenacity and change.

By the way, when I talk about courage I do not mean rashness or stupidity. Courage is not reactive, it is deeply contemplative. Rashness or stupidity are reactive knee-jerk states where there is no real sense of inner power.

Work and Flexibility

The world of work we are entering into demands that we are adaptable, that we know how to change, that we can move with agility from one set of skills to another, and that we can let go of our fixed plans and become more spontaneous. Adaptability is a core principle of evolution. We are now evolving from one mindset and identity into another. If we try and work in the new age of work with an old mindset we will struggle. We are moving into the Virtual Age, but work never stops adapting, so it will carry on evolving beyond the Virtual Age. Certainly, to enter into the Virtual Age and move beyond it is not possible with the same level of thinking that worked in the Industrial Age. Have goals but, more importantly, have vision.

Vision will take you much further than goals. Vision will help you to be more adaptable. Being adaptable means that you can shed what you do not need, you can downsize, take time out, try out new things, think outside the box, and move career paths if you desire. Be willing to let go. Now there is more room to manoeuvre and more help and support available than in previous decades.

Work and Possibility

The world of work we are entering into demands that we reclaim a sense of possibility. Liberation happens foremost on the mental level. A free mind can create a life that feels free. A trapped mind is not really aware of its true capabilities, gifts and potential. We are conditioned into being blocked by limiting beliefs and expectations. We cannot truly know ourselves or see the world through these beliefs. When we transform our beliefs, we literally see and experience a new world. My personal definition of freedom at work is to do the work we want, when we want, and where we want. In today's modern world, with all its emerging technologies, especially the internet, there is more opportunity than ever before to take charge of our time. The nine–to-five job is no longer the only option available.

Work and Talent

The world of work we are entering into demands that we bring our natural talents to it and play to our strengths. Work is a very powerful way to connect us with our gifts, talents and inner resources – often ones that we do not realize we possess. When you access a gift you lift and bless the world around you. You can be a mathematics teacher with a passion and ability for maths, which will be apparent to anyone you teach. Your passion will rub off and infect all those around you. You may be a great cook and inspire others to love cooking. You may be great with people and can find many different kinds of work that allow you to take advantage of this ability.

The important thing is that you discover your talents and apply them to a real need in the world, one which people will pay you for. You may be a latent artist, coach, doctor, engineer, healer, leader, social worker or teacher, but if you are not utilizing your talent, you will suffer.

Work and Intuition

The world of work we are entering into demands that we be more whole-brained. We cannot rely on just logic and intellect; we need our intuition and imagination to survive and thrive in these times of change. Relying on logic alone just will not do it any more. You need to become more innovative. You need to awaken your intuition and combine it with your logic. Intuition is your personal compass to navigate challenges in the workplace, find new solutions, make more empowered choices and take more effective action.

Does it make sense to only utilize half of your brain! The brain is a marvellous tool and work is one great way to use and develop it. Intuition can help you find or create the work you love. It is increasingly hard to predict what is happening in the work markets. Intuition allows you to be one step ahead of those who only proceed through logic. Intuition and logic combined form a synergy of resources that can seem almost magical.

Work and Creative Play

The world of work we are entering into demands that we are more creative, playful and available to having fun. If your work is not fun, then you need to consider changing something – either the way you work or the work itself. The old work ethic no longer really fits our current landscape. There is a new ethic emerging which is more about play than graft. This is about shifting from being a worker to a player. As a worker you know about hard graft; as a player you work in a different state of mind. Players naturally move towards what they love doing and away from what seems hard and overly serious.

Fun and play lead to being more productive and happy in your work. Play is a state of mind that is naturally creative and innovative. Play helps us to break out of our habitual thinking and doing and to try something different. Playful environments have a joie de vivre feel about them, they are lively, humorous, engaging and non-critical, and there is a genuine appreciation of good work done. Humour is an essential part of the evolution of work.

Work and Love

The world of work we are entering into demands that work is a love affair. Work does not have to be passionless – work and love are not mutually exclusive. When you are doing something you love, then it will not seem like work. Passion and enthusiasm lead to purpose – without a sense of passion we are ruled by our head and not our heart. We need the heart to be awake in our work.

We are passionate when we are working in accordance with our values. Mostly, we do not know our values, so how can we know our passion? When you work in accordance with your values you will see a different world. The world looks literally different – in fact, the world you are seeing is different to the world seen by a person who is passionless. Passion is the doorway to inspiration, where our minds are also on fire, but this fire comes from the heart. Passionate work is sensual work, it uses our hands and all of our senses.

Work and Bliss

At the other end of the spectrum from suffering comes bliss. Bliss is a state of being that is beyond joy or happiness. Bliss can come upon us unexpectedly through spiritual practice, or it can come through taking persistent steps towards doing the work we love. When we learn to flow instead of struggle, then we are on the path to bliss.

In our work we can invite grace and divine providence. All of these – flow, bliss, grace and divine providence – are spiritual concepts. Miracles can and do happen in this world. This is a mystery which we do not need to understand fully before allowing it into our lives. In the same way, we do not need to understand electricity fully before being able to turn on the lights in our home.

Work and spirituality have not really mixed for centuries, but nowadays it is more important than ever that our work is a vessel for our spirit. Work that is disconnected from our spirit can cause suffering. The good news is that nowadays we can live a spiritual life without retreating from the world. Most of the spiritual people I have met do not live in monasteries, but in varying work situations.

Bliss happens when we go beyond states of boredom, stress or fatigue, and instead learn to access states of relaxation, creativity, clarity, curiosity, focus, passion and wisdom. Work is blissful when it becomes like flowing water moving around all obstacles towards our highest visions in life and work.

Work: Intending Something Different ...

As you can see, this book explores an approach to work which refuses to accept suffering, and this new way really begins with a different focus, or set of intentions. These intentions can orientate your mind towards what you want instead of what you do not want, and this will generate more enthusiasm and desire. When you do the opposite and focus on what you do not want, depression will soon follow. Intention works with what is and what could be.

With this is mind, every chapter ends with a *Declaration of Intention*. This is a set of intentions which you can use or adapt for your own purposes, to help you clarify what you want to experience from your work today, tomorrow, next month, next year, and in the next decade. Clarity of intention is important when it comes to finding or creating work that you love.

Mostly, we do not operate with clear intentions in the world. This takes a certain amount of consciousness. Mostly, we have conflicting intentions which create conflicting results in the world. The following intentions are based on the unlimited nature of love, compassion, self-worth, and possibility. Each intention begins with the affirming phrase, 'I am ready!'

Declaration of Intention

1. I am ready to witness and transform all suffering arising from my work. I am ready to release all limiting conditioning, beliefs, assumptions, unconscious agreements, obligations, drama, persecuting, rescuing and victim consciousness that appear to block me.

2. I am ready to be more authentic, present, conscious and aware in my life and work. I am ready to release any excessive reliance on living on autopilot. I am ready to be 100 per cent courageously myself.

3. I am ready to transform my attitude and perspective in my work. I am ready to face all my fears about the present and the future. I am ready to see a bright, expansive, inviting, hopeful future opening before me.

4. I am ready to acknowledge that my time on earth is limited. I am ready to acknowledge that my time is precious. I am ready to use my time more wisely.

5. I am ready to embrace the fullness of my gifts, resources, strengths and talents. I am ready to use my intellect with my imagination and intuition. I am ready to play to my strengths. I am ready to find my niche in the world. I am ready to listen to feedback and use it wisely.

6. I am ready for fun, humour, laughter and creative play in my work. I am ready to take myself lightly.

7. I am ready for fun, playful, supportive people to enter my life. I am ready to reach out and connect meaningfully with other explorers and pioneers in my chosen fields.

8. I am ready for my work to be a love affair. I am ready to know my heartfelt values. I am ready for enthusiasm and joy to enter into my work. I am ready to love the work I do. I am ready for my life's work to be revealed to me. I am ready to dream my work into being.

9. I am ready to flow like water rather than struggle. I am ready to take effortless action in alignment with my heartfelt values. I am ready to be in the right place at the right time. I am ready for my work to unfold with ease and grace. I am ready to work with ever more bliss.

10. I am ready to take this journey and find my own way. I am ready to trust in my inner guidance and see this journey through, wherever that shall lead me.

Chapter 2

Transform Your Suffering

I teach about suffering and the transformation of suffering.

The Buddha

· ·

In the Brothers Grimm version of the Cinderella fairytale, the Prince is searching for the young woman he met and fell in love with at the ball. Although she had run away before he'd discovered anything about her she did leave one vital clue, a golden slipper dropped from her foot as she dashed down the royal staircase. 'No one shall be my wife but she whose foot this golden slipper fits,' says the Prince as he searches high and low for his beloved. Eventually he arrives at the house of Cinderella and her two stepsisters. The eldest stepsister goes first and tries on the golden slipper in her room, but it is too small for her. Then her mother gives her a knife and says, 'Cut the toe off; when you are Queen you will no longer have need to go on foot.'

A Psychological Approach to Suffering …

Putting the possibility of living past lives aside, the patterns that cause us to suffer arise primarily in our families. The false bride in the story of Cinderella is a classic case of someone forgetting their true nature to follow a path of suffering. In this case, the pattern was to marry the Prince and, thereby, save the family. This story is a great metaphor. In families there can be unresolved patterns of suffering that are simply passed through the generations – these manifest down the line as anger, inner conflict, guilt, unresolved issues and other 'entanglements'.

Why does this happen, and why do we allow it? Well, first, it is mostly unconscious and we are not aware of it, and where we are aware that something is amiss, our need for connection and belonging is so strong that we would rather endure deep suffering than experience the pain of not belonging. Our distant ancestors lived in tribal units where belonging meant the difference between life and death. In the Agricultural age, there was still a strong urge for bonding and working in community. In the Industrial mindset there came the idea that we could live independent lives without need for family or community. Yet the human instinct for belonging does not go away because we get a university education. We still, as much as ever, seek to belong to different groups and fear exclusion. No one can endure the pain of being totally alone in the world. It is for this reason that we will always unconsciously choose suffering over not belonging.

How does this work practically? Well, for instance, if your father was unhappy and struggled in his work to support his family, then out of a sense of loyalty and love, you seek to do the same. How would you feel any affinity with your father if you took a different path, one where you absolutely love your work and feel free and happy? You would have little in common. If your mother sacrificed her dreams to nurture the family, then again out of love and a misplaced sense of loyalty, you will do the same. How could you follow your dream when your mother sacrificed her dream to raise you? It would feel like a betrayal. If either parent struggled with money or in finding their passion and purpose in their work, then you may adopt that pattern out of loyalty and love for them.

Deep down there is the hope for resolution but, in practice, what happens is that the pattern just repeats down the generations. It is important to realize that when we adopt a pattern of suffering we are not being loyal to our family – we are instead being loyal to a set of ideas about our family which may or may not be true. Patterns of loyalty still operate, whether the parents are alive or not. One way to understand dysfunctional family patterns is to look at the roles they tend to create – according to some theories of Family Systems Therapy, the main roles we can adopt in the family are: the Hero, the Scapegoat, the Helper or the Lonely Child.

The Hero

The Hero is, characteristically, over-responsible and an over-achiever – the good student, the sports star, the most attractive teenager. The Hero allows the family to be reassured it is doing well, as it can always look to the achievements of the oldest son or daughter as a source of pride and esteem. On the outside, this child appears to be highly successful, self-sufficient and well-adjusted. Underneath the facade of the Hero, there tend to be strong feelings of inadequacy – and because they are usually 'successful' and tend to do what is 'right', they are often the ones that, as adults, have the hardest time admitting there is a problem.

In the film *Dead Poets Society,* a story set in a conservative boys' prep school, Neil is a student who is aiming to be a doctor. This is not really his dream, it is his father's. Neil is the classic Hero son, but wakes up through the guidance of his teacher, who encourages his students with the Latin phrase *carpe diem*, meaning 'seize the day'. Neil goes against his father's wishes and performs as Puck in a school production of Shakespeare's *A Midsummer*

Night's Dream, but his furious father finds out and immediately pulls him out of the school. Unable to make his father understand his real feelings, Neil sees no way out and ends his life.

The Scapegoat

The Scapegoat tends to act angrily, defiantly and in delinquent ways. The Scapegoat performs poorly in school, may experiment with drugs, alcohol, promiscuous sexuality, adolescent gangs, or criminal activity. The basis for this behaviour is often a deep sense of feeling hurt, ignored, and being a misfit. Typically, they may hear statements such as: 'Now look what you've done', 'If it weren't for you …', 'Now you've spoiled it for everyone.' He/she tends to act out underlying tensions and issues the family would rather ignore.

According to figures compiled by the World Health Organization the UK has the highest percentage of teenage pregnancies (classic Scapegoat) in Western Europe – second only to the United States – showing that the scapegoat is alive and kicking still in Britain. In the film *The Shawshank Redemption*, Andy is convicted of murdering his wife and her lover. He is given two life sentences and sent to the notoriously harsh Shawshank Prison. Andy is initially the classic Scapegoat, but, in time, he manages to let go of this role and escapes from prison, brilliantly turning the tables on the brutal prison governor and head guard.

The Helper

The Helper seeks to be the centre of attention, and is often hyperactive, seeking to make everyone feel better through his or her comedy and zaniness. This child takes responsibility for the emotional well-being of the family. They feel guilty that they cannot save the family. As a result, they are often attracted to the helping professions and may become a nurse, social worker or therapist. Adults stuck in this role find it easier to give love than to receive it. They often have casefiles rather than friendships – and can get involved in abusive relationships in an attempt to 'save' the other person.

In the film *Good Will Hunting* the therapist – Sean Maguire – seems to be the classic Helper. This is demonstrated in the scene where his client, Will Hunting, analyses a watercolour painting by Sean and provocatively concludes that it reflects Sean's suppressed feelings of guilt over the premature death of his wife. Sean reacts violently and grabs Will by the throat – two sides of the Helper personality!

The Lonely Child

The Lonely Child tends to be shy, solitary, and isolated in life, inwardly feeling like an outsider in the family. The Lonely Child seeks the privacy of his or her own company to get away from the family chaos. They do not want to draw attention, because they do not wish to burden the family. They tend to have a rich fantasy life, into which they withdraw. Children in the Lonely Child role sometimes gravitate towards acting and writing, since they can express hidden emotions whilst at the same time hiding behind a certain anonymity.

In the film *The Sixth Sense* the nine-year-old psychic boy – Cole – is the classic lonely child. Cole sees ghosts and is terrified by them. He is encouraged by his therapist – Dr Crow – to communicate with the ghosts and help them complete their unfinished business on earth and move on. The twist in the film is that the therapist himself is a ghost, and Cole helps him realize this so that he can move on.

These are the dysfunctional roles we can adopt as we are growing up. We may cross over and touch upon other roles at different times or stay primarily in one main role. Whenever we adopt a role we lose touch with our authentic self. When we are so disconnected we become more vulnerable to not living out the true course of our own lives.

DISCONNECTION

Disconnection leads to a number of symptoms later in life, such as:

- Difficulty in identifying and expressing feelings;
- Not stating feelings and opinions to keep the peace;
- Problems in forming and maintaining close, intimate relationships;
- Feeling a need to keep others at a distance;
- Having unrealistic expectations of self and others;
- Rigidity in behaviour and attitudes;
- Fear of taking risks;
- Feeling overly responsible for others' feelings or behaviour;
- Being overly absorbed in the needs and concerns of other people;
- Feeling guilty for no reason;
- Needing constant approval, attention or reassurance from others;
- Feeling fearful of making mistakes;
- Feeling powerless and ineffective – nothing makes a difference;
- Fear of abandonment;
- Exaggerated feelings of shame and worthlessness.

These are recipes for not knowing who we truly are or what we truly want to do in life.

. . . .

So the eldest stepsister, thinking about marrying the handsome Prince
and becoming Queen, dutifully cut off her toe. Swallowing the pain she
forced her foot into the slipper. She then went out to the King's son
who helped her onto his horse and together they rode away. It was not
long, however, before the Prince noticed blood dripping from her foot
and realized he had been deceived.

. . . .

A Psychological Approach to Transforming Suffering …

The good news is that these patterns of suffering can always be transformed,
no matter how long they have been running. Transforming them will take
some diligence and consciousness, but the effort is worth it, for beyond these
stuck roles can be found more aliveness, energy, enthusiasm and authenticity.
A great model that shows how to work with these stuck roles is The Drama
Triangle. In this model there are just three positions or roles we can play out
– the Persecutor, the Rescuer and the Victim. You could also call these roles
hero, villain and damsel in distress. This model is useful to understand and
transform patterns of suffering in the adult workplace, because it includes the
added dimension of how we as adults internalize the angry, abusive patterns,
and how we can in turn attack and blame others.

The Persecutor

The Persecutor is controlling, angry, critical and blaming of others – authoritarian, always right and perfect. This is the person that sets strict limits
and believes that attack is the best form of defence. The Persecutor gets
an adrenalin rush from anger and rage; needs to be in control and uses
verbal or physical force to stay in a position of power; deals with threats,

new ideas or conflict with anger to stay in the top position; makes self-righteous judgements about others; finds reasons to make others wrong and then creates scapegoats; believes others deserve to be punished for misdemeanours; and has a strong sense of entitlement – in other words, 'you owe me'.

The Rescuer

The Rescuer is the classic knight in shining armour, whose role is to help others. This is about feeling over-responsible for others' well-being and usually involves some form of self-sacrifice. The Rescuer loves taking the moral high ground; is stuck in a false sense of superiority; feels good at the expense of others' ability to take care of themselves; blames the Persecutor for the problem; is driven by anxiety and needs to rescue to reduce feelings of anxiety; feels guilty and selfish when not involved in other people's problems; and can become a martyr if taken advantage of by others.

The Victim

The Victim is the classic 'poor me' who plays being ashamed, depressed, hopeless, helpless, vulnerable and childish. The Victim is stuck in a false sense of being unworthy; has passive–aggressive behaviour; feels unable to take responsibility for their feelings; refuses to act as a responsible adult; oscillates between 'poor me' and blaming others; deals with threats by giving in; avoids confrontation; believes that their needs are not important; makes excuses for being a victim; and feels stuck and unfulfilled and unable to move forwards.

The Persecutor is normally in complete denial about their attacking or blaming tactics. When it is pointed out to them, they argue that attack is warranted and necessary for self-protection. The Victim looks for rescue from the Persecutor. The Rescuer fulfils this role out of a need to feel helpful and, therefore, important. The Victim, while staying in this role, cannot make decisions for themselves or take any meaningful action to end the drama. The Rescuer says, 'Let me help you,' and seeks to rescue even if others do not want or need rescuing. The Rescuer keeps the Victim in a helpless mode and, essentially, keeps giving the Victim permission to fail. (Please note that this does not describe incidents where people are being rescued from death or harm, such as a lifeguard saving a person from drowning.)

In the workplace, this triangle gets played out by countless thousands each day with painful consequences. Here's an example: the boss and a worker are having a disagreement. Boss says to Worker A that he is not pulling his weight in the job, leaving others with more to do. Worker B enters and joins the conversation by supporting Worker A. This is the starting point for the triangle. Then it may go in many different directions. Perhaps Boss will move from Persecutor to Victim, feeling unsupported by Worker B. Perhaps Worker A may then go on the attack and become the Persecutor. Later, Worker B may become fed up and attack the other two. And around it goes.

Once we are on the triangle we can rotate between all the positions in days or even hours.

We can also move rapidly around the triangle in our own minds. For example, we may be self-critical – the Persecutor – about not completing some piece of work perfectly. We may cower before this attack and spiral into the Victim – feelings of shame and self-worthlessness. When we have had enough of this we will seek to escape – the Rescuer – by justification, denial or some form of self-indulgence.

We can't get off the triangle until we recognize we're on it. Once we are more conscious of these roles we can observe how we step onto the triangle and know what hooks us on. It is useful to be aware of the costs and trade-offs for each of the three roles. Each role has its own language, beliefs and behaviour. Living as the Victim is painful. When we feel pain we seek

---

THE DRAMA TRIANGLE

1. All positions arise from denied pain, a sense of shame, and feelings of guilt and unworthiness.

2. All positions create a loss of personal power, feelings of anger and anxiety, and a sense of being stuck in dysfunctional behaviour.

---

to move away from that pain and usually the escaping behaviour creates more pain. Everyone involved in this dynamic will end up hurt and angry at some point.

Whenever we fail to take responsibility for ourselves, we end up on the triangle. Persecutors shift responsibility by blaming others for their misery. Victims look for someone else to take responsibility for them. The way off the triangle is to start to live more consciously, self-compassionately and with more self-responsibility. We unconsciously step onto the triangle and we only step off by being more conscious and self-aware.

Sometimes, just sitting with an uncomfortable feeling rather than acting on it prevents us from entering the triangle. If someone says something hurtful, you have a choice as to how you respond. An unconscious response will open a door where you step right back onto the triangle. Someone says something, this triggers an emotional response, we may then say or do something and off we go.

This is not about denying our feelings because this sets us up for any of the three positions. When we discount or deny our emotions we have a foot already on the triangle. The good news is that it does not matter whether or not others choose to get off the triangle. You can still make that choice for yourself. This choice will change the whole dynamic between you and your work colleagues. If you no longer choose to play the game and others do, then they will need to find someone else to keep the dynamic going. And getting off the triangle is not something we do once and for all. This is a process, and if you do find yourself back on the triangle, just take a breath, know your truth, forgive yourself and step off.

Transforming The Drama Triangle

Persecutor

- Stop rationalizing and justifying domineering beliefs and behaviours.
- Give up the need to be right and superior to others.
- Get honest with yourself – tell yourself the truth.
- Become aware of when you seek to get your own way and just stop it.
- Know the difference between aggression and assertion.
- Find healthier ways to release your anger.
- Take time out by walking away before you become verbally or physically abusive.
- Embrace your vulnerability instead of reacting angrily when stressed or threatened.
- Apologize to those you have harmed.

Rescuer

- Stop basing your self-esteem on helping others.
- Stop rationalizing and justifying your behaviour.
- Give up thinking that you know what is best for others.
- Address your own problems, shortcomings and negative emotions.
- Stop giving others advice, money or support.
- Suggest that others seek professional help.
- Become aware of how guilt hooks you into the drama.
- Interrupt guilty feelings by taking time out.
- See yourself as a person with healthy boundaries.
- Encourage 'the victim' to take personal responsibility.

Victim

- Stop expecting someone else to rescue you.
- Challenge any belief or thoughts that say you are unworthy and can't take care of yourself.
- Take responsibility for your feelings, thoughts and actions.
- Stop being angry at being a scapegoat.
- Start to problem solve for yourself.
- Be authentic with others and learn to state your needs clearly.
- Become aware of your 'victim speak'.
- Learn to handle confrontation and deal with other people's anger.
- Set healthy boundaries and walk away if others do not respect these.
- Look for new, positive, supportive friends.
- Define yourself as someone who is capable of handling life's problems.

A Spiritual Approach to Suffering ...

We have looked at a psychological approach to releasing suffering, so now let us turn to a spiritual approach. When the Buddha sat under the Bodhi tree and achieved enlightenment, he received some deep insights into the nature of reality and suffering. These he called the Four Noble Truths. It is interesting to note that in classic Sanskrit, the term *dukkha*, which is often translated as 'suffering', most probably comes from a word meaning 'disquiet'. The meaning of this was often described by Buddhist teachers as being like a large potter's wheel that would screech as it spun around. The opposite of *dukkha* is the word *sukha* which describes a state of being that is like a potter's wheel that turns smoothly and noiselessly. The Four Noble Truths are as relevant today in the workplace as they were in India 500 years before the birth of Christ.

The First Noble Truth

The First Noble Truth is that suffering exists. During our lifetime, we inevitably will experience degrees of sickness, injury, old age and eventually death. We may also experience psychological suffering like grief, loss, fear, hatred and frustration. Just as there is suffering, there is also ease, joy, passion and wonder. Nothing is permanent and everything is subject to the principle of impermanence. Everything will pass; one day our careers and all our achievements will pass and this is how life is. The First Noble Truth encourages us to understand and accept that suffering exists.

The Second Noble Truth

The Second Noble Truth is that there are root causes of suffering such as craving, clinging, greed and hatred. For instance, when we pursue transient things such as fame, prestige, popularity and wealth, we inevitably suffer. We can be attached to many things, experiences, memories and outcomes – ideas and opinions, a belief in being right, a role, a false sense of self, and habitual behaviour – that cause suffering. There are many ways that we suffer, and The Second Noble Truth encourages us to understand the causes of our suffering.

The Third Noble Truth

The Third Noble Truth is that the transformation of suffering is attainable. When we learn how to transform craving, clinging, greed and hatred, we can awaken into higher states of peace, compassion and bliss. The Third Noble Truth encourages us to understand that beyond suffering, freedom, well-being and bliss are always possible.

The Fourth Noble Truth

The Fourth Noble Truth is that there is a path that can transform suffering. This path is the middle way between extremes. This is the eight-fold path of liberation.

> *The truth is that our finest moments are most likely to occur when we are feeling deeply uncomfortable, unhappy, or unfulfilled. For it is only in such moments, propelled by our discomfort, that we are likely to step out of our ruts and start searching for different ways or truer answers.*
>
> **M Scott Peck**

Pain is Mandatory, Suffering is Optional ...

We may think that suffering and pain are one and the same thing, but suffering is not the same as pain. In this world pain is mandatory, you cannot escape it – there is the pain of birth, of illness, of loss, of old age and of death. However, suffering is how we relate to pain. If we avoid it, deny it or suppress it, then we inevitably suffer. We may have a fear of redundancy and worry about it for years for no reason. Then, one day, it unexpectedly happens. In the time leading up to the actual event we have created a whole fictitious story around redundancy. This story says that redundancy is bad and should be avoided at all costs; it creates years of suffering. The actual experience of redundancy might be quite different, perhaps even a liberation from a job that was not that exciting. There may be some pain felt with the actual redundancy, perhaps shock or grief, but these can be released quickly if embraced and felt. Then again, we could use this same pain – if we so choose – to feed the story and make it bigger. We could berate ourselves or complain about our lot for many years afterwards.

Facing pain rather than denying it prevents the pain from turning into long-term suffering. Pain that is acknowledged can be helpful. For instance, in his late 30s Carl Jung went through a major crisis in his life. It happened at the start of the First World War. Jung became overwhelmed by emotions and images from his unconscious and felt that the ground was falling from under him. Finally, he had an image from his childhood of making things out of wood blocks and stones. The memory was so full of emotion that he decided to follow it, so he began to play again with blocks of wood and stones. He did this during his lunch hour and at the end of the day when his patients went home. During this time he built a model village, recorded his dreams and fantasies and made sculptures and drawings. This period of his life lasted for three years. He later said that it was the most important time of his life which laid the foundation for his future work.

There will often be times in life when we feel discontented about what we are doing or where we are heading. Perhaps we cannot even really articulate this sense of unhappiness, but it is there, niggling us in the background. What we do with this sense of discontent determines our future. We can suppress it, pretend it away or address it. If we do not address it, the discontent can grow into deeper forms of suffering. When Carl Jung experienced discontent he trusted that it was happening for a reason, and this opened him up to a whole new phase in his life. He could so easily have avoided, resisted or suppressed these feelings of discontent.

When it comes to pain, using pain killers is not the solution; they become part of the problem. You may have heard about the Boiled Frog Syndrome. The basic idea – which sounds cruel – is that if a frog is placed in boiling water, it will jump out, but if it is placed in cold water that is slowly heated, it will not perceive the danger and will be cooked to death. Fortunately, according to modern-day biologists, this story is not true; a frog placed in water that is gradually heated will actually jump out. Hopefully, this is true also of human beings!

Just as a candle cannot burn without fire,

we cannot live without a spiritual life.

The Buddha

A Spiritual Approach to Transforming Suffering …

The Buddha went from a life of luxury and self-indulgence in his palace as a young prince to one of self-denial as a wandering ascetic before he was enlightened. According to one legend, he gave up the way of self-denial when he heard a group of temple dancers singing a song: 'Fair goes the dancing when the sitar's tuned; Tune us the sitar neither low nor high; The string overstretched breaks, and the music flies; The string overslack is dumb, and music dies.' The Buddha took the lyrics to heart and immediately renounced the path of excessive asceticism.

After his enlightenment, this became the teaching of The Middle Way, the path of moderation between extremes. The Middle Way is a way of wisdom and discernment that leads us between the duality of right and wrong and the extremes of stressful and dull work, uncertain and stuck work, and aggressive and driven work. In everyday life it is the way between self-sacrifice and self-indulgence, and living a modern lifestyle and spiritual practice. This is not about any ultimate destination – rather it is an ongoing process, the journey of awakening and realization.

The way, given by the Buddha over 2,500 years ago to transform suffering, is the eight-fold noble path. This gives a methodology of transformation through awareness, mindfulness and right living. Although this ancient practice is Buddhist, there is no need to hold a specific religious belief, it is not a path of faith but of experience. You can be an atheist, Christian, Hindu, Jew or Muslim; it will work just the same. This path is presented in a linear way, but it is not meant to be a sequence of single steps, rather a set of inter-dependent principles, although the mind can make each step a meditation for a day at a time.

This practice is ideal as a way to change your view and behaviour about your current work. It can also open your mind to other forms of work better suited to your true nature. All the steps in some way relate to the mind, how we view the world, the intentions we make, what we focus on, the choices we make around daily actions and our livelihood, and so on. Some schools of Buddhism – Chinese and Japanese – say that an untrained mind is like a monkey leaping from tree to tree. The 'monkey mind' can be confused, disturbed, disheartened, fickle, fluctuating, hysterical, indecisive, irresolute, prone to temptations, restless, unsettled and worried. Monkey mind can create chaos – on the other hand, a trained mind is a source of great peace, compassion, inspiration and bliss. The eight-fold path is the way to purify, train and liberate the mind.

THE EIGHT-FOLD PATH

1. **Wise View** – This is about having a way of looking at the world non-judgementally. When you judge and label things, you cannot see the essential nature of the thing or person being judged. When you judge and label others, you are more likely to judge and label yourself. Practise taking all labels off yourself. Practise taking off the filters and open your eyes to truly see the essence in others. Look for the good and the light within; do not look for faults. Practise seeing the newness in situations, even if you have seen them before many times. Keep in mind the Four Noble Truths.

2. **Wise Intention** – This is about having a pure intention in whatever you do. When you are motivated out of envy, greed or malice, your actions will be always be polluted. When you are motivated out of love and joy, and out of a sense of community, others will respond to the purity of your intention. Regularly ask yourself why you are doing what you are doing, what it will give you, and how it will benefit others as well as yourself. Do not do anything that lacks integrity. Intend to know your values and the contribution you are here to make in the world.

3. **Wise Speech** – This is about developing the art of compassionate speech, and avoiding adversarial language, such as, 'We're going to kill the competition,' 'It's a dog eat dog world,' 'If you can't stand the heat, get out of the kitchen.' Avoid harmful or idle speech. Instead, practise compassionate speech. Practise saying yes and no compassionately. Practise speaking lovingly. If you cannot do this, practise neutral non-judgemental speech. If you cannot do this, practise silence.

4. **Wise Action** – This relates to the law of karma: the principle of action and reaction as described in the Bible by the phrase 'As you sow so shall ye reap.' Take actions that produce win/win situations. Do not seek to abuse, harm, humiliate or brow-beat others. Do not seek to take that which is not yours. Avoid taking intoxicating substances. Avoid working against your core values – instead, practise saying no. Act compassionately and honestly and maintain good relations with others. Take small, consistent steps towards your greater intentions. Seek to uplift others and yourself with your actions. Make your actions a reflection of your highest ideals. This way you transform your world – both inner and outer – through action. Learn to flow and take effortless action rather than engage in action that feels like a struggle.

5. **Wise Livelihood** – Wise livelihood meaning earning one's living in a way that is wholesome, legal and peaceful. The Buddha mentions four specific areas of work that should be avoided: dealing in weapons; dealing in living beings – including raising animals for slaughter, the slave trade and prostitution; dealing in meat production and butchery; and dealing in the selling of intoxicants and poisons, such as alcohol and harmful drugs. Now there are more ways to work and harm others and the planet. Ask yourself, how ethical is your current line of work? Find work that is a real contribution to society. Work in alignment with your true values. Find work that helps you realize your latent gifts and talents.

6. **Wise Effort** – We must be responsible for using wise effort because no one else can really do this for us. The energy of the mind can be used for wholesome or unwholesome outcomes. This is about developing determination to use the mind correctly. We use the mind in an unwholesome way through inappropriately focusing on lust, ill-will, worry, or things that deaden the mind. Mental energy is the force behind right effort: the same type of energy that fuels desire, envy, aggression and violence can on the other side fuel self-discipline, honesty, benevolence and kindness. Train the mind to look for beauty, compassion and tranquillity in the world. Focus on optimism and enthusiasm rather than pessimism or depression. Practise equanimity, spaciousness, possibility and expansion.

7. **Wise Mindfulness** – This is the mental ability to see things as they are, with a clear vision and clear consciousness. Be aware of your inner world of thoughts, feelings and physical sensations. Learn to be centred in your life and work. Make everything a meditation. Washing the dishes can be a meditation, as can walking or typing. Be mindful of your environment. Be mindful of the vibe with co-workers. Be mindful of the people you talk to and the actions you take. Practise an inner calm and pause before responding to the world.

8. **Wise Concentration** – This is about practising meditation. Most of us are easily distracted, and inclined to take multi-tasking to ridiculous extremes. Avoid dissipating and wasting energy on useless distractions. Put your attention on your highest values. Practise focusing the mind like a laser on a quality such as love or play. Also practise a more diffuse focus, for instance noticing, as you go through your day, all the joy in the world around you. The mind is like a lens – it can focus or have a diffused focus. Practise both.

Declaration of Intention

1. I am ready to witness and transform all suffering arising from my work. I am ready to release all limiting conditioning, beliefs, assumptions, unconscious agreements, obligations, drama, persecuting, rescuing and victim consciousness that appear to block me.

2. I am ready to be more authentic, present, conscious and aware in my life and work. I am ready to release any excessive reliance on living on autopilot. I am ready to be 100 per cent courageously myself.

3. I am ready to transform my attitude and perspective in my work. I am ready to face all my fears about the present and the future. I am ready to see a bright, expansive, inviting, hopeful future opening before me.

4. I am ready to acknowledge that my time on earth is limited. I am ready to acknowledge that my time is precious. I am ready to use my time more wisely.

5. I am ready to embrace the fullness of my gifts, resources, strengths and talents. I am ready to use my intellect with my imagination and intuition. I am ready to play to my strengths. I am ready to find my niche in the world. I am ready to listen to feedback and use it wisely.

6. I am ready for fun, humour, laughter and creative play in my work. I am ready to take myself lightly.

7. I am ready for fun, playful, supportive people to enter my life. I am ready to reach out and connect meaningfully with other explorers and pioneers in my chosen fields.

8. I am ready for my work to be a love affair. I am ready to know my heartfelt values. I am ready for enthusiasm and joy to enter into my work. I am ready to love the work I do. I am ready for my life's work to be revealed to me. I am ready to dream my work into being.

9. I am ready to flow like water rather than struggle. I am ready to take effortless action in alignment with my heartfelt values. I am ready to be in the right place at the right time. I am ready for my work to unfold with ease and grace. I am ready to work with ever more bliss.

10. I am ready to take this journey and find my own way. I am ready to trust in my inner guidance and see this journey through, wherever that shall lead me.

Chapter 3

The Reinvention of Work

The real social revolution of the last 30 years, one we are still living through, is a switch from a life that is largely organized for us, once we have opted into it, to a world in which we are forced to be in charge of our own destiny.

Charles Handy, author and business consultant

· ·

Thomas Anderson works by day as a respectable computer programmer; by night he works as a computer hacker under the alias Neo. Neo is seeking an answer to a question – 'What is the Matrix?' He works alone at home waiting for a sign, a signal – from what or whom he doesn't know. Then one night, cryptic messages appear on his computer screen, and he is contacted by Trinity who knows the riddle Neo seeks to unravel. Trinity introduces Neo to the renegade leader Morpheus who knows the answer to the question. Morpheus offers Neo a choice: take the red pill and unravel the truth of the Matrix; or take the blue pill and forget meeting Morpheus and return to the 'façade' of the everyday world.

The Matrix of Work ...

In the world of work we live in a matrix of old ideas and assumptions largely not of our making. Until we free our minds of these old constructs, we will struggle and suffer. These old constructs act like a kind of invisible force-field that prevents us knowing our true worth and capability.

Ideas are powerful. An idea can survive a human being. There are many ideas that have shaped human thinking and experience over the centuries. For instance, the religious ideas that we were 'born in sin' and were thrown out of 'the garden' have been around for millennia. The idea that the earth was flat shaped human endeavours for centuries. The idea that we marry for love, however, is a relatively new idea – mostly, our ancestors married out of social convenience.

There are also ideas and assumptions about work that have evolved over thousands of years. Our long-gone ancestors first roamed the earth as nomadic hunters and gatherers. This work was about providing for the immediate and most basic needs of the community to survive and thrive. It was a way of life that meant constant movement and interaction with the natural world. There were dangers, but our ancestors were strongly attuned to the environment and knew how to deal with these. This way of life led to a deep bond and respect for the natural world and the earth itself. Animals were revered for their spiritual power and shamans would journey with animals as allies into the spiritual worlds, bringing back guidance and wisdom. In such cultures, the earth was seen as a great providing Mother, and by and large people lived in harmony with the earth until about 12,000 years ago.

Then, gradually, over the next couple of thousand years, nomadic tribes discovered how to cultivate crops and domesticate animals, and soon many tribes began to settle down – laying the foundations for modern civilization and the diversification of work. In time, society formed around three distinct classes, those who prayed, those who protected and those who worked. Work could be physically demanding yet also leisurely. It was normal for work, rest and celebration to intermingle. This was by and large the way of life in Europe up until the 18th century.

Then the Industrial Revolution came along, starting slowly enough and quickly gathering momentum. Very soon, the landscape of Britain – where it began – was filled with steam engines, factories, canals, roads and railways. As the number of factories grew, people from the countryside began to move into the towns looking for better-paid work. It was not only adults who were called to work, but children also began working in factories and mines. Both adults and children spent most of their working hours at the machines with little time for fresh air or exercise. These were very hard times for many working people. For those that did not work there were always the harsh conditions of the workhouse. Poverty was rife and living conditions were often poor and overcrowded. Things gradually improved, and laws were passed to protect children and adult workers from the worst abuses of employers.

Then another revolution began. From the beginning of history, information could only travel as fast as a ship, carriage or horse could move, or a person could walk. In the late-19th century, radio was invented. Over the

• •

Neo, the hero in our story, chooses to take the red pill and he is quickly taken on a journey into the Matrix. Neo is shocked to discover that life on earth is an elaborate façade created by a malevolent cyber-intelligence in order to dominate the 'real' world. Neo joins the rebel resistance and is trained in many new skills. Finally, he is ready to return to the 'mental construct' of the Matrix to confront the cyber-intelligence keeping humanity trapped in slavery.

• •

next 70 years came the telephone, television fibre optic cable, the mobile phone, the personal computer, the internet, and satellites orbiting around the earth. Very soon, information could be transmitted at rapid speed. This made the sharing of ideas, knowledge and skills faster and easier. Countries that embraced this new technology increasingly moved away from the production of goods to the provision of services. The importance of manual work gradually decreased and professional and technical work became more valued. Work was no longer contained by the boundaries of any one country. The world soon became a kind of great global village.

The Matrix has Layers …

Although our world is not ruled by a malevolent cyber-intelligence, we do live in a kind of matrix. And this matrix can keep us in a certain level of unconscious slavery. Our culturally conditioned way of thinking and behaving at work comes from a mental matrix that is structured like a step pyramid – there are a number of layers. The bottom layer is the nomadic tribal way of life. We would not have been able to move to an agricultural way of life without first experiencing the nomadic lifestyle. And without the Agricultural Revolution, we would not have been able to devote the time to think about building engines and factories. Without the Industrial Revolution, the Information-Virtual Age would not have happened.

There has been an evolution of work that stretches back thousands of years. Each step is important and necessary. Can you imagine a hunter-gatherer tribe being asked to get to grips with a computer and surf the internet? There is a whole lot of stuff in between that needs to be learnt and understood. This is not just about skills and knowledge, it is about having a certain mindset or identity. Old mindsets of work are deeply ingrained in our collective psyche.

The Industrial Way of Life

A few hundred years ago, our predecessors made a huge leap, moving from an agricultural way of life to an industrial one. This was very traumatic for many – a time of joyless hard work or, even worse, the dreaded workhouse. Those that fought against the system – for instance, the Luddites – were violently suppressed, and were either killed or transported to the colonies.

You may ask why the history lesson – well, the thinking of this age created both advances and suffering, and this thinking lives on in the hearts and minds of many. The Industrial Age created a number of new ideas that still influence us today. You may have been born in the Information-Virtual Age, but your parents, grandparents and great grandparents would have worked in the Industrial Age. They would have passed their experiences, values, assumptions and beliefs down the family line.

So, what is this dated mindset about? Well, for the first time, competition became a driving principle on a large scale – there were winners and losers. There was only so much pie to go around, and if you got a big piece, there was less for someone else. This meant that one person, company or nation would win at the expense of another. For the system to work, you needed to know your place; this was an authoritarian, command–and-control way of operating. Generally, you did what you were told or else. This was a time when class still divided people. An 'upstairs-downstairs' mentality. Rules tended to be rigid and not negotiable. Stability, security and permanence were important values of this age. There was a uniformity in tasks and assignments. Work was highly repetitive, whether physical or mental. The performance of work was often compared and contrasted with peers. This was a praise-or-blame culture – it was critical, judgemental and focused on the negative. Personal worth tended to be based on achievement, appearance, performance, wealth and status. Initiative was often criticized and in some cases punished. Emotions were seen as a weakness and were discouraged. You were there to work, not to emote. Women could get away with it sometimes, but they ran the risk of being labelled hysterical and unpredictable. Men and women were treated and paid differently. This was a stereotypical way of working, where dad went to work and mum stayed at home to look after the kids. Jobs were gender specific. Men drove buses and women worked as nurses. Men were bosses and women were subservient.

The Information-Virtual Age Way of Life

We are entering a new age of work, but we are still carrying the old mindset with us to some degree. This mismatch can create friction, tension and conflict. That being said, now work is not so much about hard graft but speed and the rapid transfer of information. Rather than rigid rules, it is about flexible ways of working. It is about a cooperative win–win frame of mind and heart, instead of the old combative style. It is no longer about sitting at a desk from nine to five looking busy; in many jobs you can log on and work at home – or almost anywhere else – through the internet. Rather than being discouraged, innovation is now actively encouraged. You are encouraged to constantly improve by trying out new things. Instead of conformity, connection, cooperation and good teamwork are now important. This is about having a mindset that is adaptable, resourceful and flexible.

You are encouraged to take greater personal responsibility and control in your work. Rather than command and control, there is negotiation and agreement. Freedom and autonomy are now important. With more fluid ways of working you can work in new ways and even work for different employers simultaneously. There is a greater notion of playing to your strengths and not trying to be a good all-rounder or spending time improving your weaknesses. Rather than criticism and praise there are appraisals and agreed forms of feedback around you to help you adjust and improve your performance. The old stereotypical thinking around male and female roles is breaking down and in this fast-paced world, both parents usually go to work.

So, we are standing with one foot on the outgoing world of the Industrial

Age and another on the incoming Virtual Age. This has not been without its problems – old ways of command-and-control management die hard. From personal experience, I know the growing pains involved in moving from one way of thinking to another. The issue is not about technology or working practices primarily, but about shifting our thinking and working values. In a sense, we all have the tendency to resist change, just like the Luddites. We are still learning to navigate our way from the Industrial to the Virtual and beyond.

THE TRIBAL CONSCIOUSNESS/IDENTITY

This is the most basic way of life for human existence. There is a strong identification with a group, and a weak or non-existent sense of individual self. This is not an 'I' way of thinking but a 'we' way of thinking. Tribal consciousness can also be 'us' and 'them'. To be separated from the tribe often meant death. This is a shamanic and magical way of living in the world where everything is interconnected and infused with spirit.

THE AGRICULTURAL CONSCIOUSNESS/ IDENTITY

This is intimately connected with the land and the seasonal nature of work. This is also connected to the feudal way of thinking and working. Here, working on the land can be hard. Nothing grows by itself. Because of the communal nature of working on the land, community is important and celebrated. This is also a magical way of life where seasonal rituals to bless the fruits of the land are important.

THE INDUSTRIAL CONSCIOUSNESS/IDENTITY

The Industrial Age is about mass production. Machines and capital are necessary. People are necessary but also replaceable. This is about manipulating the resources of the earth and the secrets of nature. This was about risk-taking and competition where individuals, groups and nations sought advantage through force and aggressive trading. A job for life, stability, security and permanence are important values, as are achievement, appearance, wealth and status. Conformity is required for efficiency which is enforced by rules and punishments. Work is hard, physical and highly repetitive. Workers are there simply to perform and produce.

THE INFORMATION-VIRTUAL CONSCIOUSNESS/IDENTITY

Rather than mass production, this is about uniqueness, creativity, innovation, cooperation and connection. Speed and fast access to information are important. With the internet, information can be accessed and communicated from almost anywhere in the world. There is no longer the need to be tied to a desk or fixed location. Work now crosses national boundaries; teams from around the world can work cooperatively on projects. Good teamwork is essential. Important values are freedom, autonomy, personal responsibility, innovation, flexibility and personal control. Work contracts can reflect a more flexible way of working. Work can happen 24/7. Work can be outsourced.

The Information-Virtual Age is Evolving and Expanding ...

Work keeps changing as technology changes, and every day different types of work are going online. Many are starting to ask themselves: Why queue up at our local surgery when we could just email our doctor or do a videoconference to get some advice? Why go to a high street law firm to be charged a hundred pounds an hour for legal advice when we could see a virtual lawyer online for far less? Why pay for expensive training courses when we can learn online at our own pace, often far more cheaply? Why pay for expensive office space when we can create a virtual office or hire a virtual personal assistant which will be flexible, accommodating and accessible from almost anywhere in the world? Why buy music in our local store when we can buy it more conveniently and often more cheaply online? Why create music in a sound studio when we can collaborate and create music online? Why spend money on posting documents when we can send them across the world instantaneously?

The Information-Virtual Age Continues to Grow Exponentially ...

By the end of 2010 around:
- 800 million were active users of Facebook;
- 88 billion people a month used the search engine Google;
- 560 million used Skype;
- 175 million used Twitter;
- 25 billion tweets were sent on Twitter;
- 5 billion photographs were hosted by Flickr;
- 2.9 billion email accounts existed worldwide;
- 1.97 billion were worldwide users of the internet;
- 255 million websites were active on the net;

- 152 million blogs were being posted;
- 2 billion videos were watched per day on YouTube.

Many industries have already been hugely transformed over the past decade, including publishing, media and retail. I was intrigued to read an article about the band Tears for Fears, who were big in the 1980s. Now, 30 years on, one member of the band, Curt Smith, lives in Los Angeles and the other, Roland Orzabal, lives in England. Rather than travel and meet up in a studio they prefer to make music via Twitter suggestions, MySpace research, and emailed audio tracks. Curt Smith believes that it is actually a lot more gratifying than working in a studio. After reading the article, I checked out Curt Smith's website and discovered that I could 'Like' him on Facebook, view images on his Flickr page, check out what he is up to on MySpace, follow him on iTunesPing and Twitter, share his tracks through SoundCloud, and subscribe to his YouTube channel! Musicians can market and promote themselves. Because of the internet, bands are less drawn to playing in obscure clubs and prefer to upload songs to their websites or social media sites, where they are immediately available to a global audience of fans or potential fans. Bands can gain popularity and make money without a record deal.

Similarly, the publishing industry has been revolutionized. You can self-publish your book and avoid signing the rights over to a publisher. You can hire freelance editors, proof-readers and cover designers. You can write and edit your book on a laptop, speak your book into a hand-held recorder and send it to a transcriber to write it up for you, or use a software programme that converts your speech into text. There are also innovative ways to market your book, such as writing an article and uploading to a social media site, or a blog through sites such as Blogger or Wordpress. You can now go the print-on-demand route, meaning there are no storage costs to worry about, and no up-front printing costs. As for the retail industry, now almost any service or product can be bought online from the comfort of the buyer's own home. This is a godsend for any would-be entrepreneur who needs very little capital to start a business. You can sell anything online, from second-hand books to your ideas in the form of e-books or virtual courses. And a virtual business can be set up to run parallel to a day job until it gets up and running under its own steam.

Advantages of Working Virtually

There are many benefits of working virtually, for employees and freelancers: greater freedom and flexibility in the place and time of your work; more opportunity to work at home, thus reducing travel costs by cutting down on commuting; you can work anywhere in the world that has an internet connection; and you can choose to work for yourself and even make money while you sleep. There are also benefits for employers, such as saving money on fixed office premises and on resources such as paper and energy.

Utopia Postponed ...

The principle of Right Livelihood is about earning our living while staying true to our deepest values. The way we work can be an expression of our deepest self, or it can be a source of suffering. If we are in a business that is harmful, making it more efficient through technology will only amplify that harm to others. And if your work is a source of harm to others, then it will also be a source of harm to yourself. Technology is a wonderful thing, but it can never deliver happiness by itself. In *The Ascent of Humanity*, Charles Eisenstein writes about the failure of the utopian visions of the Industrial Age and Information-Virtual Age:

> The age of leisure and easy plenty, technotopia, is forever
> just around the corner. First it was the Age of Coal that was
> supposed to free us from labour: in the dawning Golden Age of

the 19th century, coal-fired steam-driven machines would do all the work. Instead we got the sweatshop, the coal mine, the foundry, the Satanic mills ... the eighty-hour work week, child labour, industrial accidents, starvation wages, fabulous wealth alongside wretched slums, childhoods spent in coal mines, horrific pollution, shattered communities and ruined lives. But not to worry! The Golden Age was just around the corner, thanks to electricity! Chemistry! The automobile! Nuclear power! Rockets! Computers! Genetic engineering! Nanotechnology! Unfortunately, none of these ever quite lived up to their promise.

Despite the utopian ideals of the Industrial Age, we now know that material advances come with a terrible price to people, communities and the natural environment. In the 1960s, there was the utopian view that technology and reason would heal the world and lead to a time of plenty and greater leisure. With the advent of medical and scientific discoveries and advances in technology, it seemed that we were destined for unlimited growth and prosperity – perhaps we would even start to colonize the stars! It was believed that eventually war, poverty, illiteracy and crime would be engineered out of existence. Well, all of this remains to be seen – we now realize that the internet has not freed us from work any more than the steam engine freed our forebears from physical labour.

Disadvantages of Working Virtually

On the downside, we can lose ourselves in more frantic working, and there are more distractions through endless surfing the net. With so much information whizzing around, there is of course a greater danger of information overload, burn out, emotional exhaustion and mental overload. Other disadvantages include working 24/7; constant busyness; a blurring of boundaries between work and leisure; and an over-active mind that cannot switch off.

Our hero Neo re-enters the 'mental construct' of the Matrix and confronts the sentinel agents. But despite his training they are too strong and he is overwhelmed and killed. As he slumps to the ground, Trinity is there by the side of his lifeless body in the chair outside of the Matrix. She whispers into his ear, telling him of a prophecy – that she would fall in love with 'The One' who would liberate humanity. She kisses Neo and tells him that she loves him! Neo suddenly takes an in-breath and returns to life and in the Matrix he opens his eyes and stands up. The agents turn towards him and open fire. Neo calmly raises his hands and stops the hurtling bullets in mid-air. Neo has awakened and everywhere in the Matrix he sees flowing computer code. He realizes he is 'The One' and is no longer afraid.

Beyond the Information-Virtual Age ...

Although the Information-Virtual Age has many benefits, it cannot by itself ever give us a happy fulfilled life. There is more to the equation of happiness than developing or acquiring more and more technology. Everyone needs to work – it is a fundamental aspect of human life. What makes work meaningful is the attitude we bring to the work as well as the nature of the work itself. We may practise meditation each morning and then go to work in a hostile environment where the benefits of the work to others and the planet is questionable. Then we can meditate as much as we like, but there will always be some kind of disconnect between who we are being and what we are doing in the world. The intention is to bring the inner and the outer into harmonious alignment.

Dr Clare Graves, who inspired the systems model called Spiral Dynamics, said, 'The present moment finds our society attempting to negotiate the most difficult, but at the same time the most exciting transition the human race has faced to date. It is not merely a transition to a new level of existence, but the start of a new movement in the symphony of human history.'

We know the Information-Virtual Age has not delivered on its utopian promise, but there is still reason for hope. Not because of some new technology that will come and save the planet, but through a change in our collective consciousness around work. More enlightened ideas are seeping into the workplace through coaching and training seminars. Several friends of mine work as freelance trainers in the corporate field and they tell me that more and more big business is interested in incorporating spiritual ideas. One friend was a very successful manager in an investment bank. She kept the reason for her success a closely guarded secret for many years. She was too embarrassed to talk about it. Her secret was that she used to have predictive dreams about her work. Eventually, she started to share her dreams with her colleagues. At first they thought it was something quite strange, but she was getting good results and, bankers being a practical breed, they started to get more interested in her dreams. She eventually quit banking and started to run intuition courses, but that is a whole other story.

Although we ditched our spiritual values around work during the Industrial Revolution, many books have been written that talk about incorporating spiritual values in the workplace. Perhaps the best known of these is the bestseller *The Seven Habits of Highly Successful People* by Stephen Covey. In this seminal work that has sold more than 15 million copies worldwide, Stephen Covey presents a holistic, integrated, principle-centred approach for solving personal and professional problems. These principles are now well known in most corporate managerial circles. Stephen Covey – a practising Mormon – says that our challenges in work are of a new order of magnitude and he suggests that we are moving into a new age of work, one he calls 'The Age of Wisdom'. Daniel H Pink, author of *A Whole New Mind*, says that we are heading for a Conceptual Age, which will be ruled by artistry, empathy and emotion. Pink believes that right-brained thinking will dominate and drive the new economy.

I believe a new age of work is coming; one where human consciousness will be just as important as advances in technology. I believe that a new consciousness is needed right now – one that is capable and resilient enough to handle the opportunities and challenges of the Information-Virtual Age and take us beyond that age into a new virgin landscape of work. This new age of work is about the radical transformation of suffering and the awakening into bliss. This new age of work needs pioneers, and that means you! As a pioneer, once you start to change and step away from the inertia of the majority, you will face resistance and ridicule. But there is no need to worry, as according to science fiction writer Arthur C Clarke, all revolutionary new ideas have to pass through three stages of reaction and acceptance:

1. 'It's crazy – don't waste my time.'
2. 'It's possible, but it's not worth doing.'
3. 'I always said it was a good idea.'

DO YOU HAVE A PIONEERING VISION?

Do you yearn to work:

- In a more inclusive and compassionate way of working and relating?
- In a more heart-centred and spirit-centred way?
- With more balance between doing, with being and becoming?
- With a greater appreciation for a whole-brain approach?
- With a greater realization of your talents, gifts and skills?
- With more freedom to play to your personal strengths?
- With more creativity, imagination, vision and use of positive intention?
- With more fun and play and less hard, serious work?
- With a balance of information/knowledge with patience/wisdom?
- With a balance of complexity with simplicity?
- With more flow and less struggle?
- In a more sustainable way of living and working on the planet?
- In a business/company that seeks to make a greater positive difference in the world?

Declaration of Intention

1. I am ready to witness and transform all suffering arising from my work. I am ready to release all limiting conditioning, beliefs, assumptions, unconscious agreements, obligations, drama, persecuting, rescuing and victim consciousness that appear to block me.

2. I am ready to be more authentic, present, conscious and aware in my life and work. I am ready to release any excessive reliance on living on autopilot. I am ready to be 100 per cent courageously myself.

3. I am ready to transform my attitude and perspective in my work. I am ready to face all my fears about the present and the future. I am ready to see a bright, expansive, inviting, hopeful future opening before me.

4. I am ready to acknowledge that my time on earth is limited. I am ready to acknowledge that my time is precious. I am ready to use my time more wisely.

5. I am ready to embrace the fullness of my gifts, resources, strengths and talents. I am ready to use my intellect with my imagination and intuition. I am ready to play to my strengths. I am ready to find my niche in the world. I am ready to listen to feedback and use it wisely.

6. I am ready for fun, humour, laughter and creative play in my work. I am ready to take myself lightly.

7. I am ready for fun, playful, supportive people to enter my life. I am ready to reach out and connect meaningfully with other explorers and pioneers in my chosen fields.

8. I am ready for my work to be a love affair. I am ready to know my heartfelt values. I am ready for enthusiasm and joy to enter into my work. I am ready to love the work I do. I am ready for my life's work to be revealed to me. I am ready to dream my work into being.

9. I am ready to flow like water rather than struggle. I am ready to take effortless action in alignment with my heartfelt values. I am ready to be in the right place at the right time. I am ready for my work to unfold with ease and grace. I am ready to work with ever more bliss.

10. I am ready to take this journey and find my own way. I am ready to trust in my inner guidance and see this journey through, wherever that shall lead me.

Chapter 4

Be Yourself

*Always be a first-rate version of yourself
instead of a second-rate version of someone else.*

Judy Garland

. . . .

Once upon a time, a shepherd found a newborn lion cub. He took it home, fed it with goat's milk and bred it with his herd of goats. Consequently, though it was a lion, it behaved like a goat. One day, the cub went to the forest with the goats. Then a lion appeared who roared loudly. All the goats were scared and ran away. The cub also turned to run away, but the lion called after him, 'Brother, goats flee when I roar, but why do you run away? You are like me, a lion.' The cub did not believe him. The lion continued, 'Brother, your face is like mine, your body is like mine, and your feet have paws, not hoofs like those goats. You have the tail of a lion and you have a mane on your neck – the goat does not. Come now, cast aside this silly idea that you are a goat and roar like a lion – then all will know you are a lion and not a goat.'

Cruising on Autopilot …

Planes have a system called autopilot that allows a plane to fly, for a time, without a pilot being in charge. Essentially, the system takes over and flies the plane. We can also run on autopilot. Autopilot switches on whenever we do anything habitual that does not take real thinking. We can drive a car and be thinking about the shopping. We can work on a production line and be thinking about the evening football match that will be shown later on TV.

Autopilot has advantages, which is why we have it available to us. Once we have learned something we can just do it and put our conscious attention elsewhere. We run our body on autopilot. We do not have to think about breathing or which muscles to activate to walk to work. We just think about our destination and off we go. However, when we run most of our life on automatic, we just keep repeating habitual behaviour. We are not really present to our lives, we do not notice the brilliance of the sunrise, the feel of the ground beneath our feet, the smell of the roses on the way to work. We can also run our thoughts and emotions on autopilot.

Autopilot is a great invention of nature, but we use it to great disadvantage when it comes to living and working in the modern world. We can be on autopilot most of the day and not realize it. We get up, brush our teeth, have breakfast, take the kids to school, drop the post off in the post box, go to work, and so on. All of this time you are thinking about a hundred and one other things. Perhaps about a project you need to complete at work, or a bill that needs paying. This is living on automatic. It takes us away from the present moment. It is also not a very creative or original way to live.

Autopilot really stopped being so helpful and became a way to escape reality during the Industrial Revolution when people felt disconnected from the real world around them. Working long hours in a factory encouraged autopilot. Although work is less brutal now, we have learnt to use autopilot to multitask and to escape reality when we need to. Living this way for too long is not a good idea since it leaves us with a nagging sense of emptiness and dissatisfaction.

What Binds Us to Autopilot …

Most modern-day work disconnects us from knowing our authentic self. When we forget our true self we cannot be truly present to our lives. The good news is that we can at any time decide to live in a more present, conscious and authentic way. There are many names for our authentic self – we can call it our essence, soul, or deep or true self. Many spiritual traditions teach about this eternal aspect of our nature. This is the part of us that is here to stretch and grow through both being and becoming, stillness and achievement. We often live on autopilot because we feel compelled to live a life that is not fully ours by choice. Sometimes we just seem to be going through the motions.

There is a well-known method for training elephants. When the elephant is young, a rope or chain is put around its leg so that whenever the elephant pulls, it feels the confining pull of the rope or chain. It soon learns how far it can go. By the time the elephant is grown up, it has been conditioned to give up pulling when it feels a rope or chain around its leg. The elephant doesn't know that the rope tying it to the pole can be easily broken as soon as it decides to walk away. The only limitation the elephant has is within its own mind.

Nowadays, we are tied by imaginary ropes made up of fixed ways of behaving and responding to the conditions of our lives. In corporate life there are all kinds of deadlines and rules that need to be adhered to. This is how the imaginary rope gets a little tighter. The first step towards cutting this imaginary rope is to get more conscious and present in our lives. Only then can we start to remember that there is life beyond autopilot.

BE PRESENT – BE CONSCIOUS

- Get present to what you are doing, feel the world around you through your senses.

- When you wake up spend five minutes being present to yourself by noticing the natural rhythm of your breath.

- Be more mindful when you eat your breakfast. Take your time and savour and appreciate eat mouthful. Get present to how you drink your tea.

- Be present to the way your body moves throughout the day.

- At work, notice how you feel when you sit down. Notice physical activity at work such as the touch of the computer keyboard through your fingertips.

- Pause between activities.

- Change your routine and habitual way of doing things. For example, change the way you habitually answer the phone – try not answering it immediately or at all.

- At home, reduce the activities that prevent you from being present. Reduce or eliminate TV, computer games, surfing the net, mindless chatter and unconscious shopping.

- Meditate or take time out to reflect regularly. Create a habit of stillness.

How We Run on Autopilot ...

Habitual Sense of Obligation

A manifestation of autopilot is duty and obligation. There are conventions that we feel we must follow and so we just switch on autopilot and off we go. We feel we have to do certain things, we have no choice. We have to do the shopping, we have to do the cooking, we have to go to work, we have to say I love you, we have to be helpful, we have to take care of so and so, we have to call our friends once a week. When we live this way there is little room for knowing who we truly are. All we have become is a list of things to do.

HABITUAL COMPLAINING

1. **Complaining Becomes Habitual** – The more you practise something the better you tend to get at it. Habitual complaining finds fault with everything. Fault can even be found with what is working and seems good. The longer you hang out with complainers, the more you are at risk of becoming a complainer.

2. **Complaining is Blaming** – Complaining can quickly tip into a blame mentality. This is about seeking what is wrong rather than what is right, and problems rather than solutions. Cultures of blame generate defensive and aggressive behaviour. No one likes being blamed. Here, even neutral feedback can be interpreted as blame and criticism.

3. **Complaining is No Solution** – Habitual complaining can make things seem worse than they actually are. Complaining creates a focus where people only talk about what they do not like, what they did not get, why things are unfair, and so on. Doing this is

---

Habitual Need to Complain

If we do not like our lives or work very much, then we can blame and complain on autopilot. Of course, there are times when standing up for our rights is useful since it helps to stop or rectify an injustice. This is not the kind of complaining I am talking about here. Whenever we run on autopilot we can forget – to some degree – that we are creative, talented and purposeful beings. If we forget our true nature, we will not feel able to be too courageous, or intuitive, or successful, or spiritual in our work. There is a story about a traveller speaking with the Greek philosopher Socrates. He asked, 'What are the people of Athens like?'

---

a recipe for feeling bad. Everything is seen in a negative light. This trains your unconscious mind to see the world through a negative filter. No solution can come from habitual complaining.

4. **Complaining Creates Despondency** – Not only does constant complaining make you feel bad, it also erodes the hope that things can get better. This makes people less likely to do anything to improve their situation, because of the idea that nothing is likely to work anyway. Despondency spreads. It can be brought home and there spread to family and friends.

5. **Complainers Seek Complainers** – The more you complain the more you tend to get ahead among complainers by being the most negative and suspicious. Optimists are kept out and accused of being naïve, stupid and unrealistic. Complainers can form a strong sense of identity based on complaining and can form strong bonds with other complainers.

'Tell me where you're from and what the people there are like, and I'll tell you about the people of Athens,' replied Socrates.

'I'm from Argos, and the people there are nasty, mean and spiteful.'

Socrates thought for a moment and then said, 'Then you'll probably find the people of Athens exactly the same.'

Blaming and complaining happens when we are not peaceful and when we feel powerless to shape our lives or destiny. A more vicious form of complaining on autopilot is known as the Tall Poppy Syndrome, where autopilot goes on the attack and other people of genuine merit are resented, attacked, cut down or criticized because their talents or achievements set them apart.

Habitual Need to Judge and Criticize

We are trained to be habitually critical of ourselves and others. We are trained to be problem orientated rather than solution focused. This is one reason why we have so much conflict at work. Just try telling a colleague three things that are wrong with his work and see the result! No one likes being judged. It is much better to give honest, compassionate feedback, and to learn how to appreciate others for what they are good at. When we judge a trait in others or ourselves, we are pouring energy into that trait and giving it a greater value in the world. If we judge ourselves for being weak and hold that judgement for long enough, then very soon we will identify with being weak, we will start to speak and act from that place. Not a great idea!

Habitual Need to Fight

We can learn to be habitually aggressive. We can learn to fight over almost anything, from our ideas, our rights and our needs – such as for equipment, technology, office space, or a desire for greater status or money. In a fight there is always a winner and a loser – although it is common for all parties to lose to some extent. There was a participant in one of my workshops who approached me during a break with a problem she had been wrestling with

HABITUAL SELF-JUDGEMENT

Do you judge yourself in any of the following ways?

- I am a loser.
- I am flawed.
- I am helpless.
- I am weak.
- I am not loveable.
- I cannot start anything.
- I cannot finish anything.
- My life is a mess.
- My ideas are not worth anything.
- Nothing works out.
- My life is not going anywhere.
- I am not capable.
- I do not have what it takes.
- My future is bleak.

HABITUAL JUDGEMENT ON OTHERS

Do you habitually judge others for being:

- Too hard-working or too lazy;
- An over achiever or under achiever;
- Too capable or not capable enough;
- Too clever or not clever enough;
- Too logical or too dreamy;
- Too friendly or too distant;
- Too talkative or too quiet;
- Too polite or not polite enough;
- Too playful or too serious;
- Too authoritarian/controlling or too easy going and liberal?

for some years. The issue involved a tenant in her house. She wanted him out so that she could sell the house and he wanted to stay. She had been involved in various legal wrangles and still the whole thing dragged on. She wanted to do something else with her life other than being a landlady in North London. I asked her what was stopping her from doing what she wanted and she came up with a number of reasons why this issue had to be dealt with first. I left her with the thought that she was locking her energies into a fight and could therefore only see one option as the way through, when there were probably many. We left it there. At the end of the day she had a breakthrough and thanked me. She decided to let go and get on with her life.

I have found that it is not possible to fight and be happy at the same time. Our neurology just does not allow that to happen. Next time you get into a fight, try it out and see if you can both fight and be happy. You will find that it is impossible. So, rather than fight, how about going for happiness? This is one way to switch off autopilot. One that will leave you feeling more in charge of your choices, your actions and your life. Spiritual author Gary Zukav says:

> We are evolving from a species that pursues external power into a species that pursues authentic power. Authentic power has its roots in the deepest source of our being. An authentically empowered person is incapable of making anyone or anything a victim. An authentically empowered person is one who is so strong, so empowered, that the idea of using force against another is not a part of his or her consciousness.

To Thine Own Self Be True ...

William Shakespeare wrote the immortal lines for the play *Hamlet*, 'To thine own self be true, and it must follow, as the night the day, thou canst not then be false to any man.' Being true to yourself is being in a state of congruence.

STOP JUDGING AND START APPRECIATING!

Appreciation is the perfect cure for reversing a judgemental, combative nature.

1. Think of something you judge yourself for – perhaps being too lazy, too apathetic, too pleasing, too scattered or too unproductive. Write down the judgement of yourself and why it is a bad thing.

2. Every behaviour in you is trying to do something positive in your life. Perhaps it is not getting you the results you want, but that is another matter. Find one positive reason for the behaviour. And even though you do not like the behaviour itself, start to appreciate the positive intent behind the behaviour. Perhaps laziness is really your need for rest, perhaps apathy is your way of not putting too much energy into activities you have no passion for, perhaps being pleasing is your way of valuing other people. Write all these reasons down.

3. Think of a better way that you can achieve the intention without resorting to the same behaviour. Then put this into action. Remember that small steps are easier to commit to and instigate, and they are accumulative over time.

And this is a state of being when the things you think, say and do are perfectly aligned. This is a state of deep honesty.

Sometimes, when we are faced with challenges, doubts, fears or uncertainties, we can avoid them by running on autopilot. In Buddhism, there is the idea that there is no fixed self as in the Christian concept of soul. We have no fixed personality, we are continually growing and evolving. You are not the same as you were when you were six! Being authentic is about letting go of some of the false assumptions and illusions we hold about ourselves. We may believe that we are not capable in a certain area of our lives and act in accordance with that belief. We then discover that we are capable and we shed the belief.

Being authentic is also about being congruent. We can be authentically sad or inauthentically joyful. Our authentic self may need peace and quiet from time to time, but our adaptive self may say that we should be the life and soul of the party all the time. This is one way we can get out of sync. There are, of course, many others. When we forget ourselves we start to avoid, deny, blame and generally be incongruent. Often, incongruence is easier to spot in other people. Have you ever had a salesperson try and sell you something

· ·

There is a story about a wealthy man who one evening invited his favourite courtesan to spend the night. While he was sleeping, the crafty courtesan looked around the home and found some of his money and valuables, stuffed them into the pocket of her silk gown and fled. When the man woke up he saw that the courtesan was gone and discovered what had happened. He called upon some neighbours and together they set off in hot pursuit. As they followed the woman's trail they stumbled upon the Buddha meditating in the forest. They recognized him immediately and decided to stop the pursuit for a while to ask his advice. They told the Buddha the whole story. The Buddha thoughtfully replied, 'Instead of wandering around this dangerous forest seeking a woman and some money, wouldn't it be better to seek your true self?'

· ·

when it was quite clear they didn't believe in what they were selling?

The good news is that there is a simple formula to end being incongruent. Although the formula is simple the practice can be a little challenging. Get more present to the things that make you feel uncomfortable and choose to pause and finally stop doing them. Then start to do more things that give you a sense of peace, joy and grace. If you find yourself in a situation where you know you are being incongruent, stop, breathe and do something different. Perhaps you need to start practising telling the truth, but in ways that are not offensive; after all, the point is to be congruent, not to upset all your friends or colleagues. When you believe in what you are saying and you speak it compassionately, without blaming or shaming, then people will listen to you.

When it comes to influence, congruence is very important. The more belief and conviction you have in your message, the more persuasive it will be. Being congruent is about knowing your values, what is important to you, and not doing anything that goes against these values. When you act in accordance with your values your unconscious body language and behaviour will broadcast that fact and other people will trust you. Authentic, congruent people tend to have an upbeat attitude despite all the challenges in the workplace. They may be enthusiastic about whatever they are doing and act as a positive role model for others. They have an infectious energy and this can make work more pleasant and fun for those around them.

Switch from Autopilot to Essential Being ...

One way to switch off autopilot is through the practice of mindfulness. One of the ways the Buddha taught mindfulness was to pay attention to the breath. Breathing with full awareness helps us to stop rushing around on autopilot doing and instead return to our natural state of being. This practice can return our busy minds to their natural state of serenity. The Buddhist approach is that the mind and body are connected – energy flows better when the body is erect. Our posture affects the mind. People who need to use a chair for meditation should sit upright with their feet touching the ground.

> *When the stories of our life no longer bind us, we discover within them something greater. We discover that within the very limitations of form ... is the freedom and harmony we have sought for so long.*
>
> **Jack Kornfield**

MEDITATION

The Mindfulness of Breath

One Buddhist practice which helps to switch off autopilot involves being present and mindful to your breath.

1. Find a quiet space where you will not be disturbed. Then find a comfortable position sitting upright, either in a chair or cross-legged on the floor. Make sure that your spine is as upright and straight as possible. When you sit down, the first thing you need to do is to really inhabit your body. The eyes should be shut or the gaze should be soft and downward focusing. This is about reducing sensory input as much as possible. Become aware of your breath and feel your way around your body, from your head down to your fingers and toes. Take your time to get out of your head and into your body. The whole feeling of the breath is very important. The breath should not be forced, just natural.

2. As you remain aware of the natural rhythm of your breath, notice the inhalation and how this causes your chest and ribcage to rise. Notice the pause before the outbreath happens. Notice the breath naturally leaving you. When you have breathed out, notice the pause before the cycle of

breathing starts again. Do not think or interfere with the breath, just notice your natural rhythm.

3. At the same time that you are noticing your breath, be aware of your thoughts. When thoughts come up in your mind, don't ignore or suppress them, but simply note them. Practise awareness using your breathing as an anchor. Do not worry if you lose concentration and your mind wanders. This is natural in the beginning; just notice it and bring your attention back to the breath, wherever you are in the cycle. In the beginning, the most important lesson of meditation is noticing the unruly and scattered nature of the mind.

4. In time, with practice, this meditation will help your mind soften, become still and also focused. Continue this meditation for around 15 minutes each day.

Authenticity and Values ...

One way in which we run on autopilot is when we are not working in alignment with our values. Becoming aware of our values helps us to wake up and be more present. It is easier to be present when we are working on or towards something that feels important. Our core values are those strong issues on which we will not yield. They are the bedrock of our life, our morality, our other goals and our actions.

Whether you are consciously aware of them or not, you have a set of personal values. Mostly, we never inquire into our values. This leaves us vulnerable to adopting the values of our families or peers. Realizing your values is essential in gaining a sense of direction. Values are our compass that point to true north. Gaining insight into your values can create a major change in direction – they are that important. Values can range from a

KNOW YOUR VALUES

1. Here is a list of values. Take a look through the list and feel the ones that are really important to you. This is not about thinking, but feeling. Then choose your top five:

- Abundance, adventure, appreciation, authenticity, achievement;
- Beauty, belonging, bravery;
- Challenge, commitment, compassion, competition, communication, cooperation, creativity, courage, curiosity;
- Diversity, devotion, dynamism;
- Efficiency, empathy, equality, expression;
- Fairness, family, flexibility, flow, freedom, friends, fulfilment, fun;
- Generosity, growth;
- Happiness, harmony, helpfulness, honesty, humour;
- Inspiration, integrity, intelligence, innovation, intuition;
- Joy;
- Keeping agreements;
- Laughter, leadership, learning, logic, love, loyalty;

belief in hard work and punctuality, to the more psychological, such as self-reliance, a desire for happiness, or harmony of purpose. Of course values are at work in every area of our lives and determine our choices in our relationships, well-being and work. At work, some value their independence and freedom to make decisions and prioritize their own work. Some love cooperation and enjoy working in teams. Some love structure in their work and enjoy daily routine. Some love variety and diversity in their work,

- Maturity;
- Nobility, non-violence;
- Openness, organizing;
- Passion, peace, people, play, precision, purpose;
- Recognition, reflection, reliability, respect, risk-taking;
- Silence, security, self-discipline, self-expression, self-realization, sensitivity, service, simplicity, spirituality, spontaneity, stability, stimulation;
- Variety, vision;
- Wisdom.

2. Once you have identified your top five values, write a few sentences on each, answering what makes this quality/value so important to you. If you believe something is truly important, then just say why this is so for you. If you find it hard to articulate why the value is important, this may be a sign that the value has been adopted from someone else. Please note that the answers you give need only make sense to you.

relationships or location. Some love innovation and enjoy creating new ideas, new projects or finding solutions to everyday problems.

I cannot emphasize enough the importance of knowing your values – they are important because they guide your preferences, decisions, behaviour and responses in the world. When you think about this and your career, your values are the foundation upon which most of your choices are based. Not knowing your values is a form of ignorance that leads to suffering. Adopting the values of others leads to inevitable suffering. If you value creativity and freedom and you have adopted someone else's value for order and security, then this will inhibit your primary values. This is exactly what happened to me for the first 20 years of my working life. Believe me, it created enormous conflict and suffering, made all the more difficult since I had no idea that this conflict was raging inside my mind. As soon as my values were clear in my mind my direction at work shifted and I felt happier and more congruent with my essence.

Authenticity and Compassion …

The Buddha said, 'You, yourself, as much as anybody in the entire universe, deserve your love and affection.' Compassion is a great way to switch off autopilot. You can be a garbage collector and still practise love and gratitude. You can be CEO of a successful company and practise love and gratitude to the people 'under' you. You can talk to the receptionist and really make a meaningful connection. You can be a production worker and practise love and gratitude. You can make heartfelt connections with your co-workers, learn to laugh often and make their day.

In time, you might want to play with it some more and extend this practice to other areas of your life. It might just infect your life with greater peace and joy, so be careful! One thing I have noted in my life is that it is very hard to leave a job that I have lots of negative thoughts and feelings about. This kind of work tends to follow me around. If this applies to you, then you may notice that even if we do manage to generate enough escape velocity, these same negative thoughts and feelings can pop up elsewhere. Compassion is a great way to neutralize negative thoughts and feelings. Being more compassionate with yourself will ultimately make you a more attractive person, whether you decide to be an employee, a freelancer or an entrepreneur.

Compassion does not happen when the heart is closed. Even though the heart is naturally loving and compassionate, it can remain closed if the head is overactive and there is little love in the work you do. Clare had some judgements about herself and her work. This blocked her until she learned to be more compassionate with herself. She told me, 'I've often questioned the idea that there is some "right work" in the world for me. At least, I've questioned it in my life. I always wanted to be a writer. I studied creative writing, sat in creative writing groups, wrote stories, poems and plays and sent them off to magazines and agents to try to get them published. I made vision boards and did manifestation workshops. But not much happened. And at a certain point the whole project of trying to fulfil this ambition began to feel hollow. It just wasn't flowing. At the time I was working as a corporate copywriter. Even as I write those words I still shudder! While I was trying to become a 'real' writer, my attitude to my paid work was a bit resentful. I did my job well enough, I was punctual with deadlines and conscientious about the quality of the writing. But I saw this writing as being less valuable than writing poetry or stories. It was trivial. For one client I often wrote about different types of packaging solutions. For another I wrote about concrete. Then – to cut a long story short! – I met my spiritual teacher. In connecting with this spiritual path, certain concepts that I'd always known about and even paid lip service to before became more real to me. Let go of your ego desires. Release attachment. Be of service in the world. Suddenly, the idea of letting go of my own ambition to be a writer had some kind of context. It became a real possibility for me, something that wasn't about giving up – 'I'm a failure' – and wasn't about being self-destructive either. It was about letting go of who I thought I was and allowing there to be a space. Just an empty space where some new intention might arise, something that might be completely different from writing. Or maybe nothing would arise. And that would be okay too. Once I did this, the interesting thing is I found my attitude to my corporate work changed. I would be walking around the

MEDITATION

On Loving Kindness

This meditation is called the Metta Bhavana Meditation. The word *metta* means 'love' in the sense of compassion, friendliness or kindness. The meditation happens over five stages, each of which should last a few minutes for a beginner. You can extend the time with practice.

1. Get comfortable, relax and breathe. Focus on peace, calm and tranquillity. Open to feeling loving kindness for yourself. Expand the feeling of love in your heart. Focus on the statement: 'May I be well, may I be happy, may I be free from harm.'

2. Think of a good friend or someone that you love. Bring them to mind as vividly as you can, and think of their good qualities. Quietly focus on the statement: 'May they be well, may they be happy, may they be free from harm.' After a few minutes, focus back on yourself briefly and repeat a couple of times, 'May I be well, may I be happy, may I be free from harm.'

3. Now think of someone you feel neutral about. They may be someone you do not know well. Again, quietly focus on the statement: 'May they be

---

open-plan office of an engineering firm where I worked and the phrase "In the beginning was the Word" would pop into my head. This phrase just kept surfacing. And I began to ask myself what it would be like to write up an engineering project description with this phrase as my anchor. So far I have discovered a few things. It feels good to honour words, even in the most apparently trivial of contexts. It feels good to honour the people who have commissioned the words and the people who will read them. And it feels good to approach work, however apparently meaningless it may seem, well, may they be happy, may they be free from harm.' After a few minutes, focus back on yourself briefly and repeat a couple of times, 'May I be well, may I be happy, may I be free from harm.'

4. Think of someone you actually dislike. Do not get caught up in your feelings of dislike for them; instead, quietly focus on the statement: 'May they be well, may they be happy, may they be free from harm.' After a few minutes, focus back on yourself briefly and repeat a couple of times, 'May I be well, may I be happy, may I be free from harm.'

5. Finally, think of all four people together – yourself, your friend, the neutral person and the enemy. Open your heart and extend your feelings of love to these and then further, to those around you, to those you work with, to those in your neighbourhood and so on, until you extend loving kindness to the whole world. Quietly focus on the statement: 'May they be well, may they be happy, may they be free from harm.' After a few minutes, focus back on yourself briefly and repeat a couple of times, 'May I be well, may I be happy, may I be free from harm.'

in an attitude of service. I don't always find this process easy. But, for now, I recognize it as the coal-face of my spiritual practice. It's a process of letting go. Now I am no longer tied to the idea that my writing has to appear in a book, receive flattering reviews, and sell many copies to be worthwhile. Now I feel free to experience it in other ways.'

There is a Buddhist meditation practice that helps to open the heart and cultivate love, friendliness and compassion. This practice can, over time, make your heart an emotional fire that will warm you and all others

RELEASE YOUR AUTHENTIC-COURAGEOUS SELF

- Accept that you sometimes run on autopilot.
- Be aware of what switches your autopilot on and off.
- Notice how you feel when autopilot is switched off.
- Practise the beginner's mind each day.
- Know the edges of your comfort zone.
- Examine your values and make your work a high priority.
- Practise being present to uncomfortable feelings.
- Stop blaming and complaining, start appreciating.
- Practise breaking your routines.
- Practise being congruent in your thinking, speaking and doing.
- Practise being compassionate with yourself and others.
- Trust your courage, ideas, impulses, intuitions and visions.
- Trust your ability to find your own way in life.
- Take small actions every day that feed your authentic self.

around you. This practice of compassion embraces you, those you love, those you feel neutral about and also those you dislike or are in conflict with. This is a great way to restore harmony within yourself and within your working environment.

> *There are only two mistakes one can make along the road to truth:*
>
> *not going all the way, and not starting.*
>
> **The Buddha**

Authenticity and Courage ...

If you have spent your life tied to the imaginary rope for some years, then facing the prospect of being released into the 'wild' may seem a little scary. After all, what will happen when we stop blaming and complaining habitually is anyone's guess. Work is so changeable and unpredictable that it is much safer not to be running on autopilot. When faced with the 'white-water rapids' of life, it is better to be conscious.

Autopilot is a response to fear. When we feel scared we often switch to automatic. Fear can happen because of something that has happened already, such as a change of career or retirement. Fear can be about something we worry about that has not happened yet, such as a fear of rejection or failure. In terms of living more consciously and switching off autopilot, there are some simple truths about fear that it might be useful to know.

Fear will never go away as long as you are continuing to grow – it is natural to experience fear whenever you are on unfamiliar territory. In the same way, it is natural for other people to feel afraid when they are confronted with something new. When we can feel the fear but still remain conscious and present to the situation, we are reinforcing the belief that we are capable and empowered, no matter what the situation. When we feel afraid but take positive action, we usually feel more alive and resourceful as a result. When we are present to our fear we can transform it. Fear is very close to the feeling of excitement. Andrea Kay, career consultant and author of *Work's a Bitch and Then You Make It Work*, says, 'If you really, really want to have a career and work that you love, that gives you joy and a sense of purpose, you must believe this: That what you want is bigger than what you're afraid of.'

Declaration of Intention

1. I am ready to witness and transform all suffering arising from my work. I am ready to release all limiting conditioning, beliefs, assumptions, unconscious agreements, obligations, drama, persecuting, rescuing and victim consciousness that appear to block me.

2. I am ready to be more authentic, present, conscious and aware in my life and work. I am ready to release any excessive reliance on living on autopilot. I am ready to be 100 per cent courageously myself.

3. I am ready to transform my attitude and perspective in my work. I am ready to face all my fears about the present and the future. I am ready to see a bright, expansive, inviting, hopeful future opening before me.

4. I am ready to acknowledge that my time on earth is limited. I am ready to acknowledge that my time is precious. I am ready to use my time more wisely.

5. I am ready to embrace the fullness of my gifts, resources, strengths and talents. I am ready to use my intellect with my imagination and intuition. I am ready to play to my strengths. I am ready to find my niche in the world. I am ready to listen to feedback and use it wisely.

6. I am ready for fun, humour, laughter and creative play in my work. I am ready to take myself lightly.

7. I am ready for fun, playful, supportive people to enter my life. I am ready to reach out and connect meaningfully with other explorers and pioneers in my chosen fields.

8. I am ready for my work to be a love affair. I am ready to know my heartfelt values. I am ready for enthusiasm and joy to enter into my work. I am ready to love the work I do. I am ready for my life's work to be revealed to me. I am ready to dream my work into being.

9. I am ready to flow like water rather than struggle. I am ready to take effortless action in alignment with my heartfelt values. I am ready to be in the right place at the right time. I am ready for my work to unfold with ease and grace. I am ready to work with ever more bliss.

10. I am ready to take this journey and find my own way. I am ready to trust in my inner guidance and see this journey through, wherever that shall lead me.

Chapter 5

Work Beyond Belief

We are what we think. All that we are arises with our thoughts. With our thoughts, we make the world.

The Buddha

· ·

Some disciples went to the Buddha and said, 'Master, there are living here many wandering hermits and scholars who are in constant dispute. Some say that the world is infinite and eternal and others that it is finite and not eternal. Some say that the soul dies with the body and others that it lives on forever. What, Master, would you say concerning them?' The Buddha answered, 'Once upon a time there were a number of blind men who came across an elephant. One felt the head of the elephant, another felt its ears, another its tusk, another its trunk, another its leg, and so on. The blind man who felt the head said that an elephant is like a pot. The blind man that felt the ear said an elephant is like a winnowing basket. The blind man who felt the tusk said that an elephant was like a ploughshare. Each of the blind men came up with a different answer.'

Our Limiting Beliefs About Reality ...

We have seen that we need to update our thinking around work. Now we can go a little deeper into the personal matrix that holds us back – this matrix is what we believe about ourselves, our place in the world, our abilities, options and possibilities. We have internalized much old nonsense from the old matrix of work that has come down to us through our families and culture. What we have internalized needs to be released because it will at times seem to block us and, at worst, it can even try to literally kill us – and I am not joking! I remember some years ago, when I first started work in the City, a very tragic incident involving a young woman who jumped out of an office window to her death. No one knew why she jumped, but I would guess that she unfortunately had lots of poor-quality thinking about the quality and direction of her life. She probably had repetitive toxic thoughts that her life was not worth living. Although not everyone goes as far as taking their own life, many people at work suffer from toxic self-attacking thoughts and feelings about a whole range of stuff from not feeling good enough or smart enough to not feeling loved or appreciated. In some cases these critical thoughts are so toxic that they become lethal.

But why does this happen? A mathematician called Alfred Korzybski coined the phrase 'The map is not the territory'. What this means is that the objective physical world and our internalized perception of the world are different. What we believe about reality is not reality itself! We all have different maps or versions of reality, which means that we each literally experience a different world. Zen author and teacher Thich Nhat Hanh expresses this from the Buddhist perspective: 'If you have been to Paris you have a concept of Paris. But your concept is quite different from Paris itself. Even if you've lived in Paris for ten years, your idea of Paris still does not coincide with the reality.' You can have a map of reality that says basically people are loving and supportive, or one that says people are self-centred and only act out of self-interest. Or you may have a map that somehow combines the two! You can have a map that says 'I am a worthy person and I live in a world of opportunity,' or one that says 'I am not a worthy person and opportunities never come my way.' These maps filter the data coming to us from the world via the five senses.

These filters accept, distort, generalize and delete information. This means that you are not seeing the real world, just a certain version of it. A person with a hateful internal map will see a hateful world. Imagine the internal map of a terrorist – what kind of world do they imagine around them? A person with a loving internal map will imagine a loving world; they may have loving friends and see where the world can do with more love. They may be moved towards compassion where there is a deficit of love. Even a successful map can stop working at a certain point if it is too rigid. Imagine that you are successful in your work. This is a great thing – congratulations, you have a positive map around work. Now imagine that you become a parent and have no experience in this yet. One strategy which is not that uncommon is to use a map that has already proved to be successful elsewhere.

Imagine that your map of reality is like a map of the underground, and that your map is pretty accurate, but some information is missing or distorted. You can use the map and by and large get around successfully, but here and there you find your journey blocked because a station is closed or a line has engineering works. But by and large the map is good enough. Okay, now imagine taking this same map and using it as a street guide. It would be practically useless. For a practical example of this, imagine that Jill is a successful organizer at work. Then Jill unexpectedly becomes pregnant and is soon to be a parent. Not having any experience of parenthood she decides to do what she knows best – be a good organizer and apply it to parenthood. Perhaps it works for a while, things are organized well, the baby has everything she needs, she is fed well, bathed regularly, and has clothes for different occasions. The baby sleeps, eats or cries just as you would expect and everything goes well; that is until it stops working. The baby wants more than a happy schedule; she wants love and attention, which is not part of Jill's good organizer map. And so the baby cries and no amount of good organization makes any difference.

People with different maps of reality often have trouble communicating and cooperating together. They have different beliefs, different expectations, different ways of behaving, different values and different outcomes. One person may believe in hard work and another in creativity and the importance of taking time out for reflection. The important thing to note is that there are no right or wrong maps, just ones that help us get where we want to go as efficiently and as gracefully as possible. The best maps are those that are flexible and can be updated.

The good news is that our maps can be expanded and made more fluid and flexible, and can be upgraded. When we are flexible in our thinking, then our maps can be upgraded in the light of new experience. We are learning and growing and not discounting new information. We are willing to look around and see what is working for other people. We know we can always adopt strategies and ways of doing things from other people. We do not have to reinvent the wheel all the time.

The Thinker and The Prover ...

Despite the powerful impact our internal maps of reality have on shaping our lives, they are not real, they are creations of our imagination – we have hallucinated them into being. Although our beliefs are not real, their impact on our neurology is real enough. Beliefs are concepts that we hold in our brains which translate physically into a number of different neuron connections. Beliefs are created when you repeat a thought or idea over and over again. Your mind doesn't care whether it is actually true or not, it has no judgement on it, it is just accepted as a truth. That belief will be

HOW WE FILTER OUR REALITY

Generalization – This is where we draw universal conclusions based on one or more experiences. We naturally notice patterns which help us see trends and predict the future. It is also how we learn. It gets a bit tricky when we have an experience, assume there is a pattern and then create a generalization. For instance, a job may be boring, but to generalize that all work is boring is not a good idea. Similarly, a limiting belief such as 'life is unfair' can be generalized across every area of life.

Deletion – This can be useful; without it we would be overwhelmed by too much information. This is because the conscious mind can only handle so much information at any one time. It gets tricky, however, when you have a belief running such as 'I am not capable', as every compliment or word of appreciation is deleted by this filter.

Distortion – This is rarely useful; it takes events from reality and distorts them based on our own perspectives. For example, we may believe a person is trying to insult us when in reality they are not. Or we hear a conversation and then repeat it, but in doing so we alter the original intent or content of the message.

incorporated into the software programming in your computer brain. Then, as time passes, it becomes increasingly difficult to separate belief from reality. For instance, once you start believing that you are stupid, you will start to discover evidence to support that belief. In time you will think, speak and act in accordance with that belief. The belief has become reality. Of course, the opposite could be true, you could start believing that you are more capable than you previously realized. Then, as time passes, you will notice evidence that supports this new assertion. In time you would think, speak and act more capably. The belief has become reality.

DH Lawrence once said, 'The mind can assert anything and pretend it has proved it.' In Robert Anton Wilson's excellent book *Prometheus Rising*, the author sees the mind as having two main parts: a *thinker* and a *prover*. The thinker is extremely flexible, and can think any number of things. The thinker can think the earth is flat or spherical. The thinker can believe that all women are manipulative or essentially nurturing. The thinker can think that there isn't enough to go round or we live in a world of unlimited abundance. The thinker can think pretty much anything it likes.

The prover is much more predictable: what the thinker thinks, the prover proves. by sorting for evidence to support it. If a thinker thinks that all foreigners are lazy, the prover will sort through their experience to find evidence to support that idea. If a thinker thinks that all homeless people are victims, the prover will find evidence to support that idea. Whether a person considers themselves to be stupid or bright, the prover will certainly find evidence to show either to be 'true'.

When we believe something to be true we have a natural tendency to gather evidence to support that assertion and to disregard any evidence to the contrary. And we will not even consciously realize that we are doing it. In 1910, Ralph Waldo Trine declared:

> The optimist is right. The pessimist is right. The one differs from
> the other as the light from the dark. Yet both are right. Each is
> right from his own particular point of view, and this point of
> view is the determining factor in the life of each. It determines
> as to whether it is a life of power or of impotence, of peace or of
> pain, of success or of failure.

These ideas are backed up by an interesting experiment conducted in the 1960s called the 'blue-eyed/brown-eyed' exercise, which was created by teacher and anti-racism activist Jane Elliott. The exercise happened over the course of two days. On the first day she announced that blue-eyed children were superior, backing up this idea with a pseudo-scientific explanation. She gave them extra privileges like second helpings at lunch, access to the new jungle gym and five minutes extra at recess. She offered praise and encouragement to the blue-eyed children for being hard-working and intelligent. At the same time, she would put down children with brown eyes, saying that they were naturally lazy and stupid and less likely to succeed. She even made brown-eyed children wear ribbons around their neck. The blue-eyed children displayed arrogant and unpleasant behaviour to their 'inferior' classmates. However, at the same time, the blue-eyed children's grades improved, and mathematical and reading tasks that seemed outside their ability before were now being completed. The 'inferior' children also transformed – becoming more passive and subservient, and at the same time their academic performance suffered. Brown-eyed high-flyers were now stumbling over simple questions.

The following day, Jane Elliott reversed the exercise, making the brown-eyed children superior. Now it was the turn of the blue-eyed children to wear ribbons around their necks, and to be taunted and bossed around by the brown-eyed children. At the end of the day she explained the point of the exercise, the blue-eyed children were told to take off their collars and the children cried and hugged each other. She had not told her pupils to treat each other differently, only that they were different. Jane Elliott had shown how ideas can be quickly absorbed by a young mind, and the dramatic effect on behaviour and performance. On the positive side, she had also proved that the impact of limiting ideas can be unlearnt as quickly as they are learnt.

> *It is not the strongest of the species that survives, nor the*
> *most intelligent that survives. It is the one that is the most*
> *adaptable to change.*
>
> **Charles Darwin**

Four Steps – Transform Your Limiting Beliefs

Limiting beliefs keep us stuck in dead-end, abusive jobs because we think we have little or no choice. A belief is simply a set of frozen ideas that keep us in habitual states of thinking and feeling. These habitual psychological states keep us saying and doing the same things over and over again. A belief is nothing more than a thought or an idea that you hold to be true. Beliefs are the ideas you unquestioningly commit to, and support. They are the assumptions, views and opinions that you have accumulated and endorse. What you believe is what you stand for. The good news is that you can change your past by changing what you believe.

Step One – Know Your Old Conditioning …

You came into this world as a great light. Mostly our parents were too busy or distracted with their lives to see our greatness. As we have seen, our upbringing can open us to patterns of suffering. When it comes to what we believe, most of this is shaped in our formative years. And we are very loyal to these beliefs. As we grow up we receive many messages about possibility, capability and deservability. These are very important when it comes to work. If we grew up with the limiting message that there are very few possibilities available to us, and we believed it, then this message can negatively influence our entire working life. If we grew up with the limiting message that we are not very fortunate in the brains department, and we believed it, then this will negatively influence our ability to think, learn, innovate and move decisively

NEGATIVE FAMILY CONDITIONING

Become aware of your negative family conditioning. Remember a time when:

- Your mother gave you a negative message around your capabilities?

- Your mother gave you a negative message around your deservability?

- Your mother gave you a negative message around money or work?

- Your father gave you a negative message around your capabilities?

- Your father gave you a negative message around your deservability?

- Your father gave you a negative message around money or work?

- A grandparent gave you a negative message around your capabilities?

- A grandparent gave you a negative message around your deservability?

- A grandparent gave you a negative message around money or work?

in life. If we grew up with the idea that we should be grateful for small mercies and not expect too much, and we believed it, then this will lower our expectations about what we can do. Perhaps our parents never articulated any of these messages directly, but we receive them anyway indirectly. A positive or negative message can come through a moment of awkward silence, a certain look, or through a knee-jerk reaction to something.

POSITIVE FAMILY CONDITIONING

Become aware of your positive family conditioning. Can you remember a time when:

- Your mother gave you a positive message around your capabilities?

- Your mother gave you a positive message around your deservability?

- Your mother gave you a positive message around money or work?

- Your father gave you a positive message around your capabilities?

- Your father gave you a positive message around your deservability?

- Your father gave you a positive message around money or work?

- A grandparent gave you a positive message around your capabilities?

- A grandparent gave you a positive message around your deservability?

- A grandparent gave you a positive message around money or work?

Steve's father told him on a number of occasions that he should never be trusted with electrical stuff. He can never remember how his father came to believe this about him, but nevertheless he began to believe it over time and had a few real disasters with some home DIY. This went on for some time until he realized that this was nothing more than parental conditioning. We are encouraged or discouraged by our parents in a thousand small ways that, in time, can add up to strong conditioning. Steve went onto to revoke this conditioning, and although he never chose to pursue a career as an electrician, he is less accident prone when it comes to doing his own minor electrical repairs.

Step Two – Know Your Current Beliefs …

You must make your beliefs conscious before you can change them. Some beliefs are very strong in 'blocking' us from moving forwards. These are like magnets that hold many other limiting beliefs in place. Negative beliefs filter our experience and prevent us from moving forwards and doing anything radically different in our work. Remember that what you believe will be mirrored by reality. If you experience being 'blocked' in any way, then you will hold beliefs around being 'blocked' at work. If you are experiencing any form of limitation in your work, then you can be certain that you believe in that limitation also. Your beliefs are the glue that holds the reality together.

There has to be a match between your beliefs and the environment. If you believe that work is a 'dog eat dog' world, then you will find the perfect way to sustain this belief. If you believe that you have to be invisible to be safe in your work, then you will seek out the perfect environment for this to happen.

Lydia felt invisible in her work, but this did not prevent her from being bullied. In fact, it seemed to attract it. Because she felt invisible she felt little support around her and did not really feel like reporting it. She had some counselling and was encouraged to change the way she viewed herself at work. Over time she found the courage to reverse the thinking that she needed to be invisible and she took action to end the bullying. On the other hand, if you believe that work is a creative space, then you will find the perfect work to sustain this belief. If you believe that work is a cooperative and supportive place, then you will find an employer that matches this belief. You will not accept a reality that does not conform to your beliefs.

LIMITING BELIEFS ABOUT WORK

Take a look at this list of limiting beliefs and note which ones resonate as being true for you now. On a scale of 1–10 where 0 is 'not at all' and 10 is 'yes completely', mark each belief.

- I cannot be my true self at work.
- I cannot imagine myself doing anything better.
- I do not know what I really want to do.
- I am unemployable.
- My ideas or opinions are not welcomed.
- My dreams and passions have no space in my life.
- I do not believe I can do what I want to do.
- There is little support for my dreams.
- Work is about sacrifice and duty.
- I have no practical skill, gift or talent.
- I am not creative or innovative.
- My work does not fit who I am.
- I am lucky to have this meaningless job.
- I am not capable of changing my direction/work.
- I have no time to think, imagine or re-train.
- I am the wrong gender to do what I want to do.
- I am the wrong class to do what I want to do.
- I am not qualified enough to do what I want to do.
- I do not have enough money to do what I want to do.

- I am too old to do what I want to do.
- I am not smart enough to do what I want to do.
- I am 'blocked' by others from doing what I want to do.
- I am 'blocked' in doing what I want to do by my negative karma.
- I was born unlucky.
- Nothing works out well for me.
- No one understands or appreciates me.
- I have 'sold my soul' to the company.
- Corporations are intrinsically evil.
- My boss/colleagues never understand or appreciate me.
- I am not safe at work; to survive I become invisible.
- I am not safe at work; to survive I have to fight my corner.
- Work is always about juggling demands.
- Work is always dull and boring.
- Work is always stressful and hard.
- Work is always serious, never fun.
- There is no flexibility in how, where or when I work.
- There is no real communication or cooperation happening.
- The most important thing about my work is the money/pension.
- There is no place for my intuition or imagination in my work.
- There is no place for my spiritual values at work.

Do not believe in anything simply because you have heard it. Do not believe in anything simply because it is spoken and rumoured by many. Do not believe in anything simply because it is found written in your religious books. Do not believe in anything merely on the authority of your teachers and elders. Do not believe in traditions because they have been handed down for many generations. But after observation and analysis, when you find that anything agrees with reason and is conducive to the good and benefit of one and all, then accept it and live up to it.

The Buddha

Step Three – Reframe Your Beliefs ...

No matter how limiting your family conditioning and present thinking, your old beliefs can be changed. The good thing about the past is that it is over. You will find that once you change your thinking you will more readily be able to access internal resources to overcome challenges and move towards what you want to achieve. You can reframe your thinking about anything in your life. For example, let's say that you have just got fired from your job; you probably feel bad when you think about this. Reframing such limiting thoughts will enable you to gain a wider perspective and see positive aspects of the situation. Damien, a good friend of mine, had the interesting habit of being fired from most of his jobs when he was younger. He did not mean to get fired, but there was part of him that just could not bear dull jobs. On one occasion, he was working in a video store and when he went home he forgot to lock up. That night the store was stripped of every video. The next morning, yes, you guessed it, he was fired. Some years later he became a coach and public speaker and started giving presentations to entrepreneurs. He uses these stories as funny reminders of how even the most unlikely skill

EXERCISE

Reframe Your Beliefs

1. From the previous exercise, choose three beliefs that seem to now limit you.

2. Gather and write down as much evidence as possible that each of these beliefs is false. You are looking for factual counter examples, however small. You will notice that the more you look for this evidence the more you will find it. Counter examples to your limited thinking are everywhere – you have just filtered them out of your experience.

3. Write down three empowering statements that contradict your three limiting beliefs. Write these statements as present tense rather than future tense, e.g. 'I am open to love and support in my life.' Write these as positive statements, e.g. 'I release the past,' rather than 'I do not want the past to interfere in my life.'

4. Against each statement, gather and write down as much evidence as possible that the statement is true. You are looking for factual examples, however small. You will notice that the more you look for this evidence the more you will find it.

5. Finally, start to take small actions on your empowering statements. Remember that small steps are easier to commit to and instigate, and they are accumulative over time.

---

of being fired can come in handy in the right situation. Reframing is a great way to turn around your thinking and step onto a firmer platform where more effective action can take place.

Step Four – Practise the Beginner's Mind …

Start to move beyond what you think you know and instead practise the beginner's mind. This is a practice that comes from Zen Buddhism. The beginner's mind is a state of intense curiosity. Here, pre-conceived ideas are put aside and the mental stance of 'I don't know' is adopted. This is because living with 'I know' is a tremendous handicap that keeps us from truly knowing the possibilities held within the present moment. The 'I know' stance keeps us living in the past. It doesn't allow us anything new – no surprises, no insights, and no discoveries. People don't allow themselves this stance of 'I don't know' often enough. When we think we know something, often it is about the past and nothing to do with the present moment. What they know is their past impressions and judgements and conclusions regarding a situation that is happening now. This happens on training courses sometimes, when a participant says, 'Yes, I know that, I have done it before.' Yet in this moment it is not like what has gone before.

When we adopt a beginner's mind to things we have done before, very often something new emerges. A new insight, realization or choice. Living with 'I know' is a tremendous handicap that keeps us out of the present, and living in the past. Living with 'I know' is really about clinging to a cherished opinion or belief. And these are the fixed ways of looking at life that keep us coming up with the same conclusions. If you have been doing a job for many years you might think that you know all there is to know about it. You might even think that you are an expert in a certain field. I have always had trouble with this word. Everywhere there are experts willing to tell us about stuff ranging from the weather to parenting. Although I love hearing wisdom, I have a healthy distrust of experts. What is expert wisdom today can seem like folly tomorrow. I remember one great expert gaffe by a BBC weatherman in the late 1980s. A woman rang the BBC and said a hurricane was on the way. During a live broadcast the forecaster mentioned the call and reassured the public that everything was okay and that no storm was going

PRACTISE THE BEGINNER'S MIND

- Start to take nothing at face value, and adopt a healthy scepticism.

- For every deeply held conviction ask yourself, 'How do I know this is true?'

- Practise a sense of adventure and wonder, even with things you have done before.

- Pretend that you have never drunk tea or smelt a rose and do it as if for the first time.

- At work adopt a mindset of curiosity and play.

- In your daily do something different every day, however small.

- Learn one new thing each day at your work.

- Listen to other people's points of view, particularly ones you have not agreed with before.

- Find one positive jewel in your conversations with your colleagues.

- Take the time to talk with strangers.

- When commuting read something you would not normally read.

- Outside of work, practise learning something new each day.

- Adopt a beginner's mind with people you have known for a long time.

- Find out something about your partner you did not know before.

- Learn to embrace the unknown.

to hit Britain. The next day one of the worst storms in 300 years devastated south-east Britain.

Practising the beginner's mind is about putting aside any preconceived ideas. When you let go of the 'I know' stance, this allows the space for something new to emerge. The beginner's mind recognizes that the intellectual thinking mind has its limits. When the intellectual mind is given a well-deserved rest, new ways of thinking and relating can arise, such as 'You have an interesting point of view,' 'I have not heard that before,' 'that is so interesting,' 'I would like to find out more about that,' and 'I can't wait to try that out.'

The 'I know' stance can lead us to the delusion of adopting an 'expert' mindset. At its extreme it thinks in terms of 'If I am right, then you must be wrong,' 'I have tried that already, it does not work,' 'That is a total waste of time,' and 'They will be so impressed by what I have to say.' I know it is trendy to call yourself an expert nowadays, particularly if you want to attract clients to your 'expert' service, but there is a real danger in adopting this mindset. A beginner's mind is a place of adventure and discovery. Paradoxically, it is a place of both innocence and great wisdom.

Work Beyond Belief …

Up until the early 1950s, the sporting world did not believe that a human being could run a mile in under four minutes – such a feat was deemed impossible and beyond human endurance. On 6 May 1954, the English athlete Roger Bannister became the first person to break the four-minute mile barrier. It was a historic moment. What is not so widely known is that 46 days after Bannister broke the record it was broken again. Over the next 10 years it was broken 300 times, an average of once every 12 days. Bannister had refused to work within the confines of the belief of the impossible four-minute mile. Thus he was able to break through the commonly held belief

. . . .

There is a story about the abbot of a once famous monastery that had fallen into decline. He was troubled since the monks were no longer very attentive in their daily spiritual practice. Novices were leaving and lay supporters were deserting the monastery. The abbot decided to go on a trip to seek the council of a famous sage. On meeting the sage he told his story and the sage replied, 'The reason your monastery has languished is that the Buddha is living amongst you in disguise and you are not honouring Him.' The abbot hurried back, his mind in a turmoil. The Buddha was at his monastery? Who could he be? He thought of one brother, but remembered he was lazy. He thought of another and remembered he was dull. Then he remembered that the Enlightened One was in disguise. What better disguise than being lazy or dull-witted! He called the monks together and revealed the words of the sage. The monks were taken aback and looked at each other with suspicion and awe. Not knowing who was The Chosen One, they all agreed that they should treat each other with the respect that was due to the Buddha. As they did so, very soon the faces of the monks began to change and soon after that the monastery began to feel vibrant once more. As news spread, many novices and lay supporters started to return.

. . . .

in the limit of a human to run at such a speed. What was once felt to be impossible is now something commonplace.

This example from athletics shows how our thinking and believing can limit our performance and natural capabilities. Since performance is an intrinsic aspect of all work, this principle can be applied anywhere. When you reverse negative beliefs, you start to raise the bar in your consciousness around what is possible. Without your 'not-possible' filter on, you will see a different world. Perhaps you start being more imaginative or inventive. Perhaps you start trying out things that you would never have considered before. When you reverse negative beliefs, you start to raise the bar in your consciousness around what you are capable of doing. Perhaps you realize that there are talents that you can develop, or new skills you can learn. Perhaps you never thought yourself capable of learning a foreign language or a set of computer skills and now you realize that there is nothing stopping you. When you reverse negative beliefs, you start to raise the bar in your consciousness around your deservability. Perhaps you do deserve to do work that you love, you do deserve a fulfilling and meaningful career, and you do deserve to be paid well for what you do. How about starting to believe in yourself, in your career and in your journey through life?

WORK BEYOND BELIEF

To work beyond what you know, here is some good advice from author Stephen Covey:

Body – assume you've had a heart attack, now live accordingly.

Mind – assume the half-life of your profession is two years, now prepare accordingly.

Heart – assume what you say about another they can hear, now speak accordingly.

Spirit – assume a 1-2-1 visit with your Creator every quarter, now live accordingly.

Declaration of Intention

1. I am ready to witness and transform all suffering arising from my work. I am ready to release all limiting conditioning, beliefs, assumptions, unconscious agreements, obligations, drama, persecuting, rescuing and victim consciousness that appear to block me.

2. I am ready to be more authentic, present, conscious and aware in my life and work. I am ready to release any excessive reliance on living on autopilot. I am ready to be 100 per cent courageously myself.

3. I am ready to transform my attitude and perspective in my work. I am ready to face all my fears about the present and the future. I am ready to see a bright, expansive, inviting, hopeful future opening before me.

4. I am ready to acknowledge that my time on earth is limited. I am ready to acknowledge that my time is precious. I am ready to use my time more wisely.

5. I am ready to embrace the fullness of my gifts, resources, strengths and talents. I am ready to use my intellect with my imagination and intuition. I am ready to play to my strengths. I am ready to find my niche in the world. I am ready to listen to feedback and use it wisely.

6. I am ready for fun, humour, laughter and creative play in my work. I am ready to take myself lightly.

7. I am ready for fun, playful, supportive people to enter my life. I am ready to reach out and connect meaningfully with other explorers and pioneers in my chosen fields.

8. I am ready for my work to be a love affair. I am ready to know my heartfelt values. I am ready for enthusiasm and joy to enter into my work. I am ready to love the work I do. I am ready for my life's work to be revealed to me. I am ready to dream my work into being.

9. I am ready to flow like water rather than struggle. I am ready to take effortless action in alignment with my heartfelt values. I am ready to be in the right place at the right time. I am ready for my work to unfold with ease and grace. I am ready to work with ever more bliss.

10. I am ready to take this journey and find my own way. I am ready to trust in my inner guidance and see this journey through, wherever that shall lead me.

Chapter 6

Reclaim Your Time

Wake up. Life is transient. Swiftly passing.
Be aware of the great matter. Don't waste time.

Buddhist proverb

· ·

Once upon a time there was a hare who believed he could run faster than anything else alive. Then one day, a tortoise challenged the hare to a race. The hare squealed with laughter. 'There's nobody in the world that can win against me, I'm too fast.' So the race was on and a course was planned. The next day at dawn the hare and the tortoise stood at the starting line. The signal was given and the race began. The hare watched as the tortoise trudged slowly off. Full of confidence the hare raced down the track leaving the tortoise far behind. When the hare looked back and saw how far behind his rival was he decided to have a quick nap. 'He won't catch up with me,' he said. 'I'll have forty winks and then carry on the race shortly.'

Living and Working With Artificial Time ...

Before the British Industrial Revolution our ancestors lived by 'natural time', where time was measured by the rising and setting of the sun and the movement of the seasons.

The family of my ex-wife, Ana, come from the island of Madeira. I have been there many times and it was once an agricultural island with very little in the way of modern technology. The variety of flowers and fruit grown there is amazing. At the lowest altitude are figs, oranges, lemons and grapes. Just above sea level are banana and sugar cane. At higher levels can be found cherry, apple and plum trees. Land has for centuries been worked mainly by hand and grapes are still trodden in the traditional way. And there are regular festivals to celebrate the harvests and other important times of the year. I remember once volunteering to build some stone steps in the garden of a relation. The work was very physical since the garden was steep and long. I remember the joy of that work and how it was such a change from working in an office. There I was, in the clear open air under the golden rays of the sun. Time seemed to pass slowly and enjoyably. Back at work in London I was immediately disconnected from the natural cycles of nature.

Most of us work in offices, cubicles, factories and various workspaces shut away from nature, where our lives are ruled by the ticking of the clock. Clocks really came into their own with the Industrial Revolution, when time was money. The clock was a perfect metaphor for how scientists believed the universe operated. Mother Nature was simply a vast machine – with natural laws that kept things running in a rational, orderly manner. Despite the ideas of science, time is a mystery. Science has many unanswered questions about time. Yes, time is linked to universal forces such as the earth orbiting the sun. We know it is morning because the sun rises and brightens our day.

Yet time is also intangible; it is a construct of the mind. We can remember a personal past and imagine a constructed possible future. The strange thing is that our past is also constructed. Our beliefs filter out how we remember the past. This is why people remember past events differently. For instance, imagine there was a meeting last week – one person remembers it being a great meeting, that they came away feeling elated and how well on track the meeting was going. Another remembers how bad the meeting was, and that they came away feeling bored and disillusioned.

Time seems to slow down or increase in relation to our psychological state. Einstein, when asked to explain his theory of relativity, said, 'Put your hand on a hot stove for two seconds and it seems like two hours. Sit with a beautiful girl for two hours and it seems like two minutes. That's relativity.' It is sad but true that for millions time passes painfully slowly at work, with much clock watching and much elation at 5pm.

Your Time is Precious …

We work – this is an inescapable fact for the vast majority. Do you realize how many hours you will work over your lifetime? Well, it may shock you to know that over a lifetime you may work anywhere between 70,000 and 100,000 hours! This is a big chunk of time, and is too much to waste doing work that has little joy or meaning. So many people just keep going bravely on until something happens to make them rethink how they use their time.

If you have ever had a serious illness you would realize that your time is too precious to waste. Yvette got breast cancer for the first time at the age of 31. Up until that time she led a very hectic working life managing a marketing department for a leading London publisher. She was devastated. 'Why me, and why so young?' she asked herself, 'I just don't have time to be ill.' She remembered that when the consultant told her she would have to come in for surgery the following week, she told him in all seriousness that it was impossible as her assistant was going to be on holiday. Fortunately, the consultant ignored her protests, and she was admitted a few days later. The illness proved to be a turning point in her life. Before the illness, dancing, her real passion, had played second fiddle to her publishing career. After the illness she realized that she had to follow her heart and put dancing first.

The bow kept forever taut will break.

Zen saying

The Dis-ease of Busyness ...

From the day we are born we are bombarded with messages that being busy is good. Busyness is an illness we have inherited. The interesting thing is, I have never heard of anyone saying on their deathbed that they wished they had spent more time at work. Our time gets lost in busyness. And the thing is that busyness is usually not very productive. When people feel too busy they feel stressed and are more likely to make mistakes. Sometimes, slowing down can actually improve productivity. Yet how often do we get told to slow down and take our time to really do a good job!

In the Information-Virtual Age everything is still about speed. Now we have to be busy and also do everything at top speed. Even in the Industrial Age there was the notion that Sunday was a day of rest – and perhaps worship and prayer – and that mealtimes were an opportunity to spend quality time with your family. Now that is mostly gone, we work 24/7 and quality time with the family is an interesting ideal, but not always a reality. As the pressure on our time increases there are many things that start to drop off the 'to do' lists. When it comes to quality of living, speed is not always a good thing.

In Timothy Ferris's book *The 4-Hour Work Week* he makes the distinction between being effective and being efficient. He says effectiveness is doing the things that get you closer to your goals. On the other hand, efficiency is about doing tasks, whether important or not, in the most economical manner possible. Very efficient people may be doing stuff that does nothing to make the organization more effective. For instance, you may be great at selling books, but if the market is moving away from hardcopy books to virtual e-books, then it does not matter how good you are at selling books, ultimately you will lose your job. You may be great at compiling reports, but if those reports do not help the company in any meaningful way, then you are being efficient but not effective. A friend of mine owned a training company selling services into the corporate world. The company was not doing well. I had a chat with their office manager and was shocked to discover that she spent most of her time compiling reports, all of which simply outlined how badly the company was doing and was likely to do in the future. I wondered, how many reports do you need before you take action? A much better use of her time would have been to stop compiling reports and instead use the time to think of ways to improve trading results.

The Thieves of Time ...

When you do not like what you are doing, the thieves of time can take many forms.

Overwork

A severe thief of time is busyness and overwork. Not only do tired employees make more mistakes, but overwork leads to stress and tension. Research tells us that long-term overwork can lead to exhaustion which is detrimental to physical and mental health. You're no good to anyone, least of all yourself, if you're not in good mental and physical condition. The higher up this problem occurs in an organization, the more likely it will be to cascade down into every area of the business. When the CEO is tired and unhappy, those around him will tend to feel it also. This is not good for the individual or the company. The car manufacturer Henry Ford learned in the mid-1920s that by cutting the workday from ten hours to eight and the working week from six days to five, he could increase total worker output and reduce production costs. So overwork really does not pay!

Multitasking

Another thief of time is multitasking. Here we are called upon to do more than one task at a time and we need to switch between tasks. This is like being a plate spinner in the circus. They spin lots of plates on sticks and the only thing keeping them up is the momentum of the spin. The moment the spin decreases the plate begins to wobble. Unless respun quickly, the plates will crash to the floor. So you are working on a couple of projects, the phone keeps ringing, emails are pinging into your inbox at a steady rate, as you head off for a dinner date your cell phone goes off, and so it goes on. Welcome to the world of the multitasker.

One very useful principle in terms of time management and multitasking is the 80/20 principle. This principle was created by Vilfredo Pareto, an Italian engineer, who first came across it when he observed that 20 per cent of the pea pods in his garden contained 80 per cent of the peas. He went on to observe that 80 per cent of Italy's wealth was owned by 20 per cent of the population. In the last decade this has been popularly known as the 80/20 principle, partly due to the work of Dr Joseph Juran in the 1930s and 1940s, who worked with a principle he called the 'vital few and trivial many'. He found that in any activity a few – 20 per cent – aspects are vital and most – 80 per cent – are trivial. The value of the Pareto Principle is that it reminds you to focus on the 20 per cent that matters. Of the things you do during your day, only 20 per cent really matter. Those 20 per cent produce 80 per cent of your results. And there are 20 per cent of things that can steal 80 per cent of your time.

HANDLE BUSYNESS AND MULTITASKING

- Avoid having too many activities, ideas or projects on the go at once.

- Learn to prioritize your ideas and your tasks, and finish one thing at a time.

- If you have 'To Do' lists, make them short and list items in terms of priority.

- Distinguish between what is important for you and what is important for others.

- Identify the 20 per cent of tasks that you need to focus on.

- Practise saying yes and no.

- First thing in the morning, focus on just these tasks.

- When working turn off all other distractions such as phone or email.

- If an interruption is important keep notes so you can pick up the thread later on.

- File away stuff that has been done or is no longer important.

- Plan your day in blocks of time with certain blocks kept open for flexibility.

- Take regular breaks; practise staying balanced, centred and sane.

Sensory Overload

Another thief of time is information and sensory overload. Today, the average person is exposed to more information in one day than many of our ancestors were in a whole lifetime. Most of us are bombarded with information from

STOP SENSORY OVERLOAD

- Start to restrict the amount of information coming in.

- Stop watching so much television. Limit it to an hour or so a day at most. Stop reading so many newspapers, magazines and books. Read one book or magazine at a time.

- Limit the amount of time you spend on the computer. Stop playing computer games. Stop surfing the internet and stop idly chatting on social networking sites.

- Take regular breaks and stretch. Have a cup of tea and really enjoy it. Give your brain a rest. Practise silent meditation and allow your thoughts to unwind a little. Sit in nature, enjoy the peace and quiet and also the healing sensations of flowers and sunshine. Take time for pleasure such as a sensual massage.

dawn till dusk. This is especially true if you live and work in a city. We are surrounded by TV, radio, iPods, newspapers, magazines, advertising, conversations, noise and smells. We live in a world of soundbites and tweets. We can be overwhelmed with so much imagery, sound and sensation. Our conscious mind is like a computer hard drive; it only has a limited amount of processing space. When that is exceeded we start to feel confused, tired and scattered and we cannot concentrate.

Procrastination

One way to lose time is to procrastinate over unimportant stuff. Three hundred years ago the English poet Edward Young wrote, 'procrastination is the thief of time'. Procrastination will steal your time and your energy. Putting things off requires lots of mental energy – the more you put things off

---

STOP PROCRASTINATING

Typically, a lengthy 'To Do' list will increase the chances of procrastination. It results in a sense of guilt, and overwhelms you. On the other hand, I have found that shrinking such 'To Do' lists tends to increase a sense of enthusiasm and resourcefulness.

- Keep your list of things to do at a manageable level.

- Be realistic about how long these will take – do not crowd tasks in too short a time.

- Make a conscious effort to minimize the list of things you have to do.

- As far as possible, do not let others impose unnecessary tasks on you.

- Sometimes you put things off because some of the tasks are waiting for solutions. Learn to be solution-focused, widen your perspective, research how others have found solutions in similar situations, and seek out advice or help.

---

the more you have to worry about later. And there is always the danger that the stuff you are putting off today will build up and become a crisis tomorrow.

Learn to Delegate ...

To be effective, there are times when you need to delegate work, particularly if you have a managing or leadership role. No one can do everything and it is all too easy to get lost in the minutiae of detail and lose focus on the bigger picture. As a boss, the benefit of delegating is that it eases work

TIPS FOR DELEGATING

1. **Be Clear**. Know what you want to achieve. Know what you want others to do. Also, be clear about how you are going to use the time you have freed up.

2. **Express Clearly**. Be clear in your communication; let others know what you want. Be specific. Communicate your goals. Give clear instructions. Communicate your expectations. Set realistic deadlines.

3. **Get Out of the Way**. Trust the people you delegate to. Avoid micro-managing. Let them do it in their own way. Allow for the resourcefulness of others to surprise you.

4. **Follow Up**. Delegating doesn't mean letting go completely. Follow up to make sure the job has been done.

pressure and increases time for more important tasks. The most common reasons why people do not delegate are: a belief that no one else can do it as well or as fast; that others cannot be trusted; that they will make a mess of things; that it will take too long to train people; or that training others will make you more dispensable.

I once knew someone who managed an organization, but who had most of these beliefs. After about a year his stress levels were so high that he went to the doctor who prescribed medication for stress and depression. Another six months was all it took before he left the job. Thank goodness the next person in the role knew how to delegate and create a cooperative working atmosphere. The important thing about delegation is that it is not about assigning routine tasks to anyone who happens to be available. Tasks have to be considered alongside strengths, weaknesses and previous experience of all available personnel.

Own Your Time …

Beyond managing your time you can start to own your time. One way is to work more virtually. This can free you up to work part of your working week at home. Some jobs are more suitable to this than others. Most office-based work can be done virtually.

Things to consider before seeking to work more virtually are how well you currently manage your time; how easily you are distracted; how organized you are; how easy you find it to overwork or procrastinate; and how important it is to you to work face to face with other people. As a virtual worker there will no quick catch-ups with colleagues around the coffee machine or water cooler. You need to be more proactive in arranging meetings and networking to avoid feeling isolated.

Another important factor to consider is the importance of recognition and appreciation for work done. It is easier to feel appreciated when face to face than through a congratulatory email. One way to begin to try it out is to work virtually for, say, one day a week and see how it feels. The challenge is to convince the boss that it is an effective way of working; it has to suit all parties for it to really work and be a long-term effective way of managing your time.

As a freelancer or entrepreneur, working virtually is often ideal. It allows you to work more flexibly and to save on the need for a physical office space. Then your office is your laptop and your mobile phone.

At the age of 16 Brigit was 'packed off to college to take a horse management course' as she was 'too dim' to do A levels. After two years running around in jodhpurs and smelling of manure, she realized that this was not the life for her. She got a job as a secretary and progressed through the company during the next four years from secretarial work to accounts, then to technical support and finally to sales. By the tender age of 22 she was regularly flying around Europe giving presentations. Brigit told me, 'I'd finally found something that I could do – it was new, exciting, not a woman's world, and I wasn't dim.' It was the mid 1980s and the PC revolution was taking off. She got a job selling IBMs and Compaqs. After two years the expensive offices, huge marketing budget and massive bonuses took the company into receivership and Brigit found herself out of a job. But this was a great opportunity, since she had a solid client base which had also been let down by the company going bust. She started helping clients with technical support and training, which made her realize that she could set up a viable business doing this type of work. Twenty-five years later she has a thriving, successful business. I asked Brigit what she most loves about her work. She said, 'With the wonders of remote technology I can work on client systems from my rural home and I now tend to spend every other week visiting my London clients. My work is flexible so it also allows me to travel. I take three months out every year to travel. Every morning I wake with a happy heart and it stays in that state for the duration of the day.'

And so we left the hare about to take a nap. And nap he did – he fell fast asleep and was snoring happily as the sun started to sink below the horizon. Meanwhile, the plodding tortoise had made it almost to the finishing line. Then the hare woke with a jolt. He saw the tortoise far off in the distance, leapt up and raced down the track as fast as he could go. But the hare's final dash was just too late, and the tortoise beat him to the winning post. Tired and in disgrace the hare slumped down beside the tortoise. 'Slowly does it every time!' said the tortoise.

Be Present, Open and Still ...

In China each morning, millions of elderly Chinese gather in parks to practise tai chi, the ancient Chinese martial art that involves mostly slow, fluid movements. This is very different kind of exercise than that promoted during the 'no pain no gain' physical exercise era. These movements are gentle and tend to have a healing and restorative effect on the mind and body. tai chi is widely practised in Asia because of its ability to reduce stress, improve posture, and increase chi or energy, stamina, flexibility and balance. Since it is quite suitable for anyone of any age, I was intrigued why young people seemed mostly uninterested. I asked a Chinese friend and she told me that younger generations are not interested because they do not have the

---

BE PRESENT, BE OPEN, BE STILL

Be Present – Practise being present with everyone you meet, from the checkout person in the supermarket, to people you casually meet on public transport, to your work colleagues. Take time to connect and stop rushing; take time to talk to others; avoid interrupting and encourage others to say what they are thinking.

Be Open – Refrain from telling people what to do and how to do it; ask questions rather than offer solutions; explore different ways of looking at an issue; and practise the art of real listening.

Be Still – Take time out to do nothing very much; learn different ways to meditate; have long hot baths; take long walks in nature; notice the stillness and beauty around you; smile at flowers; hug a tree; take up yoga or tai chi; or learn to doodle.

time, they have to work. This is a pity since tai chi is a great practice if you want to learn how to be present, open and still. But if you do not have time to learn tai chi there are other ways to become more present and centred in your life.

Slowing Down Time …

Sometimes it is useful to slow down time if it seems to be going too quickly and running out. How is that possible? Well, as previously stated, time is both connected to force and gravity in our external world and also a mental construct. As a mental construct you can slow down your experience of time. Imagine for a moment that you are on the bridge of the USS Enterprise, and taking a lift down to one of the holodecks. You step into the room and around you is a computer-generated hologram of a forest. It is very dense and green and sunlight streams down from above, illuminating the floor of the forest. Here there are unusual insects and many beautiful butterflies of different sizes and colours. You tell the ship's computer to slow down time and as you look everything is in slow motion – the wings of the butterflies gently flap around you. Then you tell the ship's computer to freeze the scene and the butterflies stop in mid flight. With your imagination, in the same way, you can alter how you experience time. This is how the unconscious works; it can slow down your experience of time.

There are occasions when it is useful to slow down inner time. For instance, if you are enjoying an experience and it seems to be going too fast, you can slow down the inner experience and learn to savour each moment more fully. You can even freeze certain 'negative' thoughts that are causing you to suffer in some way and imagine that they explode into a thousand pieces. This is a great way of communicating to your unconscious mind to start filtering out such thoughts.

E X E R C I S E

Slowing Down Inner Time

This exercise can be used when you are feeling stressed, busy, pushed for time, have a pressing deadline, or when everything seems to be going too fast. It is good for planning a future event where you would like to slow down your experience of time.

1. Remember a time in the past when time went really slowly and really pleasantly. Perhaps you were somewhere beautiful and you could feel everything around you – how the place felt, smelt, sounded and looked. As you remember this, notice how you feel in your body. This is how you experience slow, enjoyable time.

2. Now notice this sensation, notice where in the body you are feeling it. Then imagine expanding it all over and around your body. As you do this, notice how pleasant this feeling is. As you do so, notice what colour this sensation is. As you think the question, your unconscious mind will present you with the answer – you do not have to think too much. Now make this colour more vivid and beautiful and allow it to move around your body.

3. Now think of something that you are about to do that you would love to experience more as a slow experience of time. Perhaps something that was stressful in the past. Imagine it vividly.

4. Then bring in the sensation of slow, enjoyable time. Remember first the feeling in your body and then the colour of slow time. Let the feeling and the colour of slow time infuse the constructed image of the future experience. Imagine as you think of this future – perhaps as a still image or an inner video clip – that it is being infused with the colour of slow time. Watch as time seems to slow down and at the same time the feeling of enjoyment of the experience increases. Stay here for as long as you need and then come back to your everyday reality.

Take Time Out …

Susie was training to be a ballet dancer, but she felt disillusioned and had not been working for a while. I asked her thoughts on work and she replied, 'We live in a results-based culture where we feel guilty if we do not achieve. What would the experience of life be like if we could just be? We're so used to gaining or losing. "Lose" weight, "gain" a certificate. What if there was no result? The idea of spending time with no end result is fairly new to me. It is a concept I am just starting to explore. After all, what would be the point in spending time and having nothing to show. No photographic proof, no teachings of wisdom, no art.'

This used to be called taking a sabbatical. The Old Testament encouraged everyone to take a sabbatical year off every seven years. During this year off, fields were to lie fallow, debts were to be forgiven, relationships were to be repaired and introspection was encouraged. Over time, the notion of taking a sabbatical has practically disappeared. Mostly now we do not even observe a weekly Sabbath.

Belinda and Toby gave up their executive jobs, sold the big house and flashy cars and went travelling. Their kids had grown up and left home, and they wanted to develop their spiritual sides more and also do something more meaningful in life. This was a huge change in lifestyle, and leaving the UK, families and friends to taste more of what the world had to offer was a big leap. It was also a golden opportunity to explore the world, wind down from the work of the past 20 years and relax into a more chilled and steady pace. Part of the plan was to visit Peru where they attended a spiritual ritual on a mountain. Here they had a great awakening to their spiritual purpose and path in life. They had planned to travel for another year, but here they decided to move to Ibiza. They now live in Ibiza on a small budget compared to their extravagant lifestyle in England. But they love their simple lifestyle and have no wish to return to the 'rat race'.

Cheryl also went to Ibiza as a young woman, but not to take time out – rather to explore the island's reputation for being a hedonist's utopia, and a place of escape. At that time of her life it was all about having a good time. Then some years later she was diagnosed with ME and returned to Ibiza for a different reason: this time to explore the world of healing, mind, body and spirit. Without any savings, a job or a real purpose other than to find healing she went to live in Ibiza. Cheryl says, 'What followed was the most profound and transformational year of my life to date. A year in which I lived on the edge, but by the end of it I was aligned with my life's purpose, a purpose beyond myself. An inner-venture of discovery. A time of letting go of layer upon layer of fear and social conditioning. Taking the Russian doll approach and revealing the true essence of who I am. Finding out what's underneath, being true and getting to know myself.' I later discovered that Cheryl was 'coincidentally' good friends with Toby and Belinda.

Nicholas originally trained as a chemical engineer and worked for a global mobile satellite communications company as a project manager in London. Then he took some time out to go on a retreat in Spain. Nicholas told me about the moment he decided to change his life. 'I had just got up and was watching a beautiful sunrise over the Sierra Nevadas. I said to myself, "I just can't do this any more."' He knew he needed a complete break and so on his return to London he told his employers he wanted to leave, negotiated his job into a part-time position and agreed to complete all the projects he was responsible for. Then he went off travelling. He spent a lot of time in India, the Himalayas, the Andes and Central America. He eventually returned to the United Kingdom, and decided to turn his 'weekend hobby' spiritual practice into a full-time business. This happened 12 years ago and he has been running his own business doing what he loves ever since. He says, 'And I have never once regretted leaving the corporate world.'

The Chinese have a saying: 'The person who returns from a journey is never quite the same person who began it.' And this was the case for

TIME TO TAKE TIME OUT?

It may be time to take some time out when:

- You cannot remember the last time you had a break from work;
- You cannot remember the last time you went out and had fun;
- The most exercise you get is walking to the photocopier and back;
- You are thinking far too much about work;
- You are finding it hard to sleep;
- Friends tell you that you look like you need a break;
- You think you may have been working too hard;
- A project, a job or a long-standing relationship has come to an end;
- You feel tired in your bones; you feel burnt out;
- What once excited you no longer does it any more;
- You feel it is time to find a new direction in your life.

the authors of *Six Months Off* – Hope Dlugozima, James Scott and David Sharp – three journalists who took time out to write their book. They interviewed hundreds of people who had taken sabbaticals and could not find one person who regretted doing so – *not one*! They found that people who took a long break from work felt they had improved their mental health; 'recharged their batteries'; and found space to pursue new personal and professional challenges.

Declaration of Intention

1. I am ready to witness and transform all suffering arising from my work. I am ready to release all limiting conditioning, beliefs, assumptions, unconscious agreements, obligations, drama, persecuting, rescuing and victim consciousness that appear to block me.

2. I am ready to be more authentic, present, conscious and aware in my life and work. I am ready to release any excessive reliance on living on autopilot. I am ready to be 100 per cent courageously myself.

3. I am ready to transform my attitude and perspective in my work. I am ready to face all my fears about the present and the future. I am ready to see a bright, expansive, inviting, hopeful future opening before me.

4. I am ready to acknowledge that my time on earth is limited. I am ready to acknowledge that my time is precious. I am ready to use my time more wisely.

5. I am ready to embrace the fullness of my gifts, resources, strengths and talents. I am ready to use my intellect with my imagination and intuition. I am ready to play to my strengths. I am ready to find my niche in the world. I am ready to listen to feedback and use it wisely.

6. I am ready for fun, humour, laughter and creative play in my work. I am ready to take myself lightly.

7. I am ready for fun, playful, supportive people to enter my life. I am ready to reach out and connect meaningfully with other explorers and pioneers in my chosen fields.

8. I am ready for my work to be a love affair. I am ready to know my heartfelt values. I am ready for enthusiasm and joy to enter into my work. I am ready to love the work I do. I am ready for my life's work to be revealed to me. I am ready to dream my work into being.

9. I am ready to flow like water rather than struggle. I am ready to take effortless action in alignment with my heartfelt values. I am ready to be in the right place at the right time. I am ready for my work to unfold with ease and grace. I am ready to work with ever more bliss.

10. I am ready to take this journey and find my own way. I am ready to trust in my inner guidance and see this journey through, wherever that shall lead me.

Chapter 7

Be More Resourceful

If you have no legs, run.
If you have no voice, scream.
If you have no hope, invent.

Cirque du Soleil

· ·

In Washington DC, on a metro station one cold January morning, a man with a violin set up to play. He played six Bach pieces for about 45 minutes and during that time around 2,000 people passed by, most of them on their way to work. For the most part they were oblivious to the music. After 4 minutes the violinist received his first dollar – after 45 minutes he had collected a total of $32. Finally he finished and packed away. No one noticed, and no one applauded. What few people present that day realized was that this violinist had just played one of the most intricate pieces ever written for a violin – and with an instrument worth $3.5 million. Two days before this performance the violinist, Joshua Bell, had sold out in Boston where each theatre seat averaged around $100.

You Are Naturally Resourceful ...

Put a talented person in the wrong environment and they will go unrecognized. Keep them there for too long and they will forget they have any talent at all. To this end, you do not fully know what you are capable of doing in this lifetime – you do not know the fullness of your capabilities, talents and resources. This may sound a bold statement, but it is one I have come to realize is sadly true for most people.

The idea that you are talented is not a new one, though it will seem just an interesting theory if you have been brought up in a critical/drama-filled family, educated in a narrow left-brained way, and then go to work where your gifts and abilities go unrecognized and remain unutilized. When a gift is not seen it tends to stay dormant at best and at worst wither. Industrial work tends to be repetitive and is not designed for particularly talented people. The factory job does not require genius, it requires compliance. When a talent is not used it gets forgotten. Then it becomes a myth and not a reality.

It is important to realize that you are gifted, whether you know it or not. You probably know some of your gifts and talents, but you can be sure of one thing – there is so much more. You may believe that you have reached the limit of your capacity because your work demands no more of you. You may be an outstanding author, chef, engineer, manager or playwright, and have come to the end of what you can achieve in that line of work. What was a challenge yesterday is now simply a routine. I have a friend who is a successful non-fiction author. After writing non-fiction for many years he needed a new challenge. He took a month out on retreat and then came up with the idea of writing a novel. The idea immediately excited him and he got to work straight away. Writing a novel stretched him into new territory where he had to work with his creative imagination. This was a very different way of writing and he found he was good at it. The book is now published and I wish him the best of luck.

William James, author of *The Principles of Psychology*, wrote, 'Most people live, whether physically, intellectually or morally, in a very restricted circle of their potential being.' This is a form of suffering – one that afflicts millions, perhaps billions. Somewhere, we have a vague notion that there is more to life than what we are doing. Perhaps we read it in a book or an article in a magazine or newspaper. Certainly this idea is not totally new. Then there comes a moment when we may realize that we are capable of so much more. I once met a guy called Gerald who was a corporate trainer and management consultant. He was successful and also enjoyed what he did. I asked him how he got started. He said he used to work as a gardener, tending the grounds of a business college. As he went about his work he could often hear the lectures through the open windows. Then he got interested and asked, one day, if he could drop in and listen to one of the classes. The college agreed and he was hooked from then on. He gave up gardening and started attending regular lectures. Before listening in on the business classes he had no idea that business held any interest for him. And he had no idea that he would be any good at business until he got going. He heeded the calling.

You may be a naturally creative and innovative person, yet if you work in a role that is more about organizing and structure you will find it hard to realize your creative talents. You may be a natural teacher, communicator or writer, yet if you work in a job where production is more important than communication you will find it more difficult to realize and express your natural abilities.

Some work is not only the wrong kind of work for you, it actually holds you back. But it might not just be the kind of work you are doing. It might be the way you are being treated. Some workplaces treat you as less than capable, perhaps even as stupid. It is a strange but true fact that some managers choose to keep their staff in a state of perpetual unresourcefulness through constant criticism. It is a way of controlling people that really belongs to the old Industrial mindset, but can be found in plenty of modern work environments. Basically, this creates a culture of conflict and mediocrity. It is certainly hard to liberate your talents in an environment that ignores your essence and creates distractions and dramas to keep you from realizing your own talents – I call this 'being kept in an unresourceful space'.

We can be conditioned to stay in an unresourceful state. As we have already explored, this is what we call being a victim – a learned position that prevents us from really knowing our true worth and capabilities. Do you remember the children's board game, Snakes and Ladders? Well this game perfectly describes how we move from one psychological state to another. When you are in a positive state such as enthusiasm, joy or optimism you climb the ladder. As you climb the ladder, you feel more energy and vitality in your body. Your mind is clear and you feel more centred and self-assured. On the other hand, when you feel in a negative state such as anger, boredom, fear, frustration, guilt or resentment, you slide down the chute. On your way down you feel drained, weaker, confused and less capable.

The American lecturer and poet Ralph Waldo Emerson once said, 'Most of the shadows of this life are caused by our standing in our own sunshine.' There are resourceful states such as being creative, happy, motivated or relaxed. There are non-resourceful states such as feeling angry, fearful, resentful or tense. We are always in a psychological state, we 'cannot not' be in a state. As long as you are on this earth you are going to be in one state or another. Feeling rooted in more resourceful states means we tend to lead happier, more successful and fulfilling lives. In a resourceful state we can also more easily access emotions, memories, strategies, skills and abilities.

We can learn to stop feeling unresourceful and shift to feeling more resourceful. It just takes a little awareness and practice.

CHANGE AN UNRESOURCEFUL STATE

If a psychological state is causing suffering, then it needs to be interrupted. If you feel in an unresourceful state try one of the following:

- Go for a walk.

- Breathe more deeply.

- Sit with a tree.

- Listen to something humorous.

- Write or paint.

- Hit a pillow.

- Do something playful.

- Speak out your own name forcefully.

- Play some soothing, vigorous or uplifting music.

- Speak gibberish for five minutes.

- Have a friend take you somewhere unexpected.

- Speak to a stranger.

- Say some affirmations.

- Drink some hot tea.

- Recall a happy memory.

- Look out for people smiling or laughing in the street for no reason.

- Find something to smile or laugh about.

- Read a poem.

- Go for a swim.

- Do some physical exercise.

- Watch an uplifting movie.

- Go to a concert.

- Do something different – anything! Start to train your brain and nervous system to be joyful rather than depressive, and optimistic rather than pessimistic.

MEDITATION

Reverse a Negative State

This process comes from the Institute of HeartMath. You can practise this three or four times a day, as you wake, before you sleep or just before making any decision.

1. Shift your attention to your heart. If it helps, you can place a hand over your heart area.

2. Imagine that you are breathing in and out of your heart. Find a natural rhythm with your breath.

3. As you breathe, start to focus on a positive emotion such as love or appreciation. It may help to remember a time when you felt this way. Keep doing this for several minutes until you feel rooted in this state of being.

Transform an Unresourceful Workspace ...

In Yourself

If there is a problem at work, ask for help – consult a friend or mentor. Remember that you do not have to solve it alone. Remember that you are good and worthy even when you are not performing well.

In a Colleague

Do not take their lack of resourcefulness personally. Clear and authentic communication is always important. Avoid speaking in terms of general statements and judgements. Be clear and compassionate; and remember that other people are good and worthy even when they are not performing well.

In an Organization

Perhaps the organization you work for is facilitating an unresourceful space and is not aware of it. Gather feedback and support from co-workers. Is there a common goal or vision? Is there anything that needs to be communicated that is being ignored? Spend time together looking for effective solutions rather than analysing the problem too deeply.

Stretch That Brain …

We have a brain and we can either use it or not. The latest scientific evidence shows that we can train our brains to be more flexible and resourceful! Professor of Psychology Ian Robertson explains in his book *Mind Sculpture* how our brains are not 'hard wired' from birth. He reveals how new connections between previously unconnected brain cells are formed each time we do something different or learn a new skill – as we learn new skills, we really are literally 'sculpting' our minds. As Professor Robertson says, 'The human brain of all ages is plastic, that is, it is shaped by what you do, what you learn and what you think.'

There are ways that we can maintain a healthy brain. We have already looked at different psychological states; different states produce differences in our brain chemistry. For instance, low levels of serotonin have been associated with depression and low levels of noradrenalin have been associated with hopelessness. On the other hand, more positive states release dopamine to the brain and this leads to the experience of pleasure, and the release of serotonin leads to even greater levels of joy. We can encourage the release of dopamine and serotonin by engaging in pleasurable activities. Anything from a hug to making love to any form of creative expression. Here are some ideas to stretch your brain and keep it flexible and healthy.

EXERCISE

Stretch Your Brain

To keep your brain flexible choose tasks:

- That are new and surprising, that take you out of your routine way of thinking;

- That teach you something new and grab your curiosity, interest and full attention;

- That are steadily progressive, where you start at a level within your capabilities and then gradually do more challenging tasks;

- That help you use all your senses – what you hear, see or feel, taste and smell;

- That are enjoyable, stretching and rewarding, for these can amplify your ability to remember.

Open That Heart …

Being resourceful is not just about developing our brain, we also have a heart. Many scientists and researchers maintain that the heart is a 'little brain'. Dr JA Armour first used the term 'heart brain' in 1991 – he discovered that the heart has a network of neurons and neurotransmitters similar to that found in the brain. This elaborate circuitry enables the heart to act independently of the brain – allowing it to learn, remember, and even feel and sense.

According to researchers at HeartMath the heart is far more than a simple pump – it is, in fact, a highly complex, self-organized information-processing centre with its own functional 'brain' that communicates with and influences the cranial brain via the nervous system, hormonal system and other pathways. HeartMath call this the 'Intelligent Heart'.

The heart and brain actually influence one another's functioning, although the heart sends a great deal more information to the brain than the other way around. The information it sends includes signals that can influence a person's perception, emotional experience and higher cognitive functions. Researchers have discovered that by intentionally improving your emotional state you can experience greater mental clarity and heightened intuitive awareness. According to the research at HeartMath, 'it becomes clear that the age-old struggle between intellect and emotion will not be resolved by the mind gaining dominance over the emotions, but rather by increasing the harmonious balance between the two systems – a synthesis that provides greater access to our full range of intelligence.'

The heart has long been thought to be the centre of our emotions and, although in our rational world of work emotions are not always welcome, our emotions are a great treasure. Our emotions are just different forms of energy in motion within us and when we allow them to flow they can lead us to greater depths of love, joy, inspiration, passion, gratitude and serenity.

Emotional Intelligence – EQ – is a relatively recent behavioural model, rising to prominence with Daniel Goleman's book *Emotional Intelligence*. Emotional Intelligence is increasingly relevant to work because it helps to understand and assess behaviour, management styles, attitudes, interpersonal skills and potential. Your EQ refers to your ability to understand and empathize with others. EQ is your ability to use your emotions in positive and constructive ways. It's about engaging with others in a way that brings people towards you, not away from you.

Howard Gardner, a Harvard psychologist and author of *Frames of Mind: The Theory of Multiple Intelligences*, says that Emotional Intelligence is our ability to understand other people, know what motivates them and how to work cooperatively with them. EQ argues that the conventional way we measure intelligence is limited. You may have a PhD in astrophysics, but then again you may be socially inept. You may be very bright but lack the ability to know how you are feeling from moment to moment. If you lack EQ, then you will lack true depth of passion, you will not know what drives you, you will not be able to be completely transparent with people and as a result other people are less likely to trust you. Work can be a hotbed of emotions, either unexpressed or poorly expressed. Some studies show that EQ is a much more accurate determinant for success and career growth than technical skills or a high IQ.

Individuals with good EQ can look at themselves honestly and reflect accurately on their deeper intentions; be aware of emotional triggers in times of stress; know the difference between aggression and assertiveness; know when to reach out and when to be still, pause and consider before speaking or acting; and be more accountable.

Engage Your Strengths …

If there is one thing that will help to awaken our inner resources it is learning how to play to our strengths and not our weaknesses. Mostly, we are taught to focus on fixing our weaknesses. This is probably the biggest fallacy of our education system. Marcus Buckingham, co-author of *Now Discover Your Strengths*, says, 'Unfortunately, most of us have little sense of our talents and strengths … guided by our teachers, parents and managers, we become expert in our weaknesses and spend our lives trying to repair our flaws, while our strengths lie dormant and neglected.'

Perhaps the second greatest mistake we make is to learn to be a good all-rounder. This is one way to avoid knowing what we are really good at. Every successful artist, athlete, entrepreneur, politician or scientist has achieved greatness by focusing on their areas of strength. Can you imagine what would have happened if Beckham, Chopin, Einstein, Obama or Pavarotti had tried to be good all-rounders? The important thing to realize is that no matter how hard you try, it is unlikely you will ever be more than average in areas where you do not have any real aptitude or interest.

OPEN YOUR INTELLIGENT HEART

A good practice is to check in with yourself regularly through the day. Start by asking yourself, 'How am I feeling right now?' Do you feel anxious, angry or sad, excited, happy or grateful? Do you feel tense or expansive? What do you feel about your work? What do you feel about your colleagues? What do you feel about your boss? Unacknowledged feelings can block your effectiveness and happiness. Take responsibility for your feelings. The more self-aware and self-responsible you are the less others will be able to 'press your buttons'. Avoid office gossip. Pause and take a breath before responding in emotional situations. Listen more than you speak. If you feel angry you may need to communicate this cleanly – objectively, compassionately, without blame, and with a clear, positive outcome in mind. If you feel sad, then communicating this directly to the relevant party without rationalizing the feeling away can lead to new levels of authenticity and trust developing. Do not feel shy about expressing 'positive' emotions such as love and joy; when you appropriately express these openly you touch, warm and uplift those around you. Build good relationships based on a mutual support and warmth.

Perhaps the third greatest mistake is thinking we always have to get it right. We become resourceful through making mistakes. Being resourceful is not the same as perfectionism! When a child first starts to learn to walk there is the inevitable wobble and fall. What then happens is that the child gets up and does it again. Can you imagine what would happen if, when you took your first step and fell, you decided that your walking career was over!

We British tend to be quite shy and humble about our strengths – not like our cousins across the Atlantic who are trained in being more upfront. However, I asked a few friends about their strengths and eventually I managed to squeeze some interesting answers out of them. First I asked Erica, a vocation coach and trainer, about her strengths in her work. She told me, 'I would describe my strengths as the ability to explain complex theories in a simple and engaging way, that makes them relevant to people's lives and to their practical reality. I'm good at acting as a catalyst, consciously or unconsciously, to accelerate people's self-understanding, growth and motivation. Working with groups, I feel energized, centred, grounded and totally present. This is easy to do, because I have passion for what I'm sharing, passion for the transformation tools I offer and passion for the talented people in the room!'

This is the kind of clarity I recommend people find about their strengths. The interesting thing to note is that just being aware of a strength and acknowledging it in some way will tend to make it more active in your life. And I'm sure you will agree that this is a far better exercise than acknowledging your weaknesses and making them more active in your life. I asked Richard, who works with people with mental health issues and drug addiction, about his strengths and he said, 'With my clients I am empathic, supportive, non-judgemental and have good boundaries. With my colleagues I work well in a team, and am reliable and consistent in the quality and care I take in my work. What makes my job worthwhile is that 25 per cent of the people I work with recover and make progress.' Richard is now studying to become a social worker. He is probably one of the most empathic people I know.

Okay, so you now have a flavour of what I mean, let's get a little more specific around strengths. There are three broad categories of strengths: knowledge-based skills, transferable skills, and personal traits. I asked Bonnie, who works in marketing, about her strengths and she replied, 'Marketing is a hybrid of research, hard facts, knowing what has worked before, and current market trends. It can be very formulaic. What I excel at is that I am naturally innovative and intuitive and I am willing to take risks. I am good with big ideas and with the project management side which is rare, since most excel at one or the other. Also, I am good with relationships, building trust, and I know how to convince clients to come on board with my ideas.' So Bonnie has knowledge-based skills around her speciality of marketing, transferable skills such as being good with the big picture and being able to manage detail, good people skills, intuition, innovation and risk-taking. Although Bonnie did not mention that much on the personal traits side, I know from personal experience that she has a great sense of humour, is flexible, punctual, reliable, a great team player and hard-working.

Knowledge-Based Skills

These are acquired through school, college, university, seminars, or in-house job training. Examples include broad skills such as computer skills or languages, or more specific skills such as graphic design, management, marketing, public relations, human resources and so on.

Transferable Skills

These are the portable skills that you take from job to job such as communication and people skills, leadership skills, the ability to influence and guide others, organizing, problem-solving, planning skills and time-management.

Personal Qualities

These are your unique qualities such as courage, curiosity, innovation, good judgement, flexibility, focus, self-discipline, passion and reliability.

E X E R C I S E

Know Your Strengths

Answer each of the following questions in terms of your knowledge-based skills, transferable skills, and personal traits:

- What strengths do you recognize that you have in your current job?
- What strengths have you developed in previous jobs?
- What strengths do you recognize that you use outside work?
- Think of three occasions you achieved something you felt proud of.
- Think of three occasions when someone praised you for what you did.
- What feedback do others give you about your strengths in or out of work?

To find the work you love, determine what your strengths are, what you are naturally good at. Determine what you care about, what moves you the most. If you don't know what you care about, open yourself more fully to the joy and pain of the world.

Laurence Boldt

Finding a Right Fit in the World ...

If you want to feel passionate about what you do in the world and to be successful, then finding your niche is a very important part of the jigsaw. Theodor Seuss Geisel – a well-loved writer and cartoonist – is better known by his pen name Dr Seuss. To please his father, who wanted him to be a college professor, Theodor went on to Oxford University in England after graduation. However, he was bored with his academic studies and decided to tour Europe instead. After returning to the United States, Theodor began

RESOURCEFUL PEOPLE = FORTUNATE PEOPLE

For over ten years psychologist Richard Wiseman conducted a research project into luck. He researched people who experienced persistent good or bad luck throughout their lives. He worked for several years with over a thousand volunteers, examining their personality differences on a number of levels. He found that lucky people are more likely to achieve their dreams and ambitions for two reasons.

1. They expect to be happy and successful and see bad luck as being short lived; they persevere in pursuit of their dreams or goals; and they know how to turn misfortune into good fortune.

2. They know how to form and maintain relationships. They enjoy meeting and connecting with people; they use open body language that people find attractive and inviting; they smile and make eye contact more than unlucky people; they are more likely to initiate conversations and are more effective at building lasting relationships; and they create a strong network of friendships and optimize their chances of a lucky encounter.

to pursue a career as a cartoonist. He also worked in advertising to support himself and his wife through the Great Depression. During the Second World War he worked as a political cartoonist and later joined the army and worked in their propaganda-animation department. After the war he started writing children's books, but it was not until 1954 when he read an article in *Life Magazine* about illiteracy amongst schoolchildren that a light bulb went on inside of him. The article concluded that the poor reading ability of children was because of the lack of imagination in the reading books available. Theodor's challenge was to write a book that was educational that 'children can't put down'. He was contracted to write and illustrate a children's book using only 225 key words. As a result *The Cat in the Hat* was born nine months later. Theodor had found the perfect fit in the world for his love of humour and his skill as a writer and cartoonist.

By the time of his death in 1991, over 200 million copies of his books had found their way into homes and hearts around the world.

Fortunately, the world has a great need for your passion and talent. There is no end of need in the world. People need architects and engineers to build, dancers to dance, drivers to drive, doctors and therapists to heal, musicians to play, teachers to teach, writers to inform and inspire – without need in the world none of these professions would exist. Finding the right fit is like finding the right romantic partner – with the right one you feel like you have gone to heaven.

Finding a Sangha …

In Buddhism there is a concept called the *Sangha*. This is a Sanskrit word that roughly translates as assembly, company or community that has a common goal, vision or purpose. Traditionally the term *Sangha* referred to a monastic group of ordained Buddhist monks or nuns. Nowadays it tends to refer to a community of Buddhism practitioners. In the broader sense of the word it is can also mean a group of people that have a common set of interests and values, direction and purpose.

There is a great value in finding a *Sangha* on this path for mutual encouragement and support. One of my coaching clients is Natalie, a lovely, talented young woman who wanted to find her 'inner sparkle'. Since leaving university she knew she didn't want a nine-to-five career, but she was afraid to admit what she really wanted to do, which was to perform! So she temped in offices, worked in retail, in hospitality, in promotions – she did it all and was very unhappy. She would 'stand in department stores at the till in a daze, my senses deadened, thinking I know I am here to do more!'. She eventually gave in to the call and went to drama school to train as an actor. I asked her how performing made her feel, and she replied, 'When I'm in a show and surrounded by actors, there is a creative energy that I just can't get anywhere else. When I perform I get lost in a character, but in the process of finding this character I find I get to know myself better, to explore those inner emotions that normally don't see the light of day. I find it a cleansing, spiritual experience at times to use emotions and feelings that I would normally be scared to release, and that's why I know that it's my soul's purpose. When I watch a film, read a script, rehearse a scene, and get lost in theatre I literally sparkle.'

It is important for Natalie to have other actors to inspire and encourage her to pursue her own acting career. A few months after this conversation I heard that Natalie was moving to Los Angeles to pursue her acting career. I am sure she will sparkle there just as brightly. Personally, I love hanging out around creative people; they help to remind me of my own creativity. Whatever you are interested in, go and hang out with people with similar interests and passions. If you want to sing, go listen to other singers. If you are a natural comic, then go hang out with other comedians. If you want to learn internet marketing, go and find other people with this interest. If you want to stimulate your own healing or psychic abilities, then go hang out with people who have already done so. On a practical level this will help you develop your skills, but beyond that it will help you activate your inner knowing and wisdom. If you want to awaken your drive and ambition, then hang out with people who have found a driving sense of purpose. If you want to be more courageous, then hang out with people who enjoy speaking the truth.

*The next best thing to being wise oneself is to
live in a circle of those who are.*

CS Lewis

Why Find a Sangha ...

In Pamela Slim's book *Escape From Cubicle Nation* she comes up with six great reasons for connecting with other people.

They Save You Time

When you need 'a quick idea, or resource, or perspective', having a group of supporters to call upon will save you time.

They Share Resources

Resourceful people tend to explore new ideas, products and ways of doing things. Resourceful people tend to love sharing these ideas with others. And the more you share the more others will share their discoveries with you.

They Introduce You

A great way to meet new people is to be introduced to another person by someone you trust. They in turn may introduce you to other great people. This is a great way to meet some very interesting individuals in the world.

They Hold You

When entering a new project or pursuing a new dream you will encounter things you have no experience of. When faced with the new it is easy to feel anxious or to make premature decisions. Having people around with a cool head and a light touch can help prevent you making rash decisions that you might regret later on. They can help to talk you down from the cliff edge.

They Spread the Word

If you are seeking to promote your career, the right connections can help you find the right fit for your skills and talents. If you have a service or product you are selling, personal recommendation goes a long way.

They Tickle You

A group of friends and supporters can help stop you being so serious and help you laugh more at your own mistakes and foibles.

Create a Virtual Sangha ...

One of the advantages of the Information-Virtual Age is that nowadays it is very easy to connect with others around the globe through social media. You can connect with people, form groups, create physical or virtual events, and share ideas, information or insights without regard to physical proximity or timezone.

Nowadays there are hundreds of social media sites to choose from. I have thousands of 'friends' through social networking sites, particularly Facebook. I have found that many of my virtual friends pop up in this world also. I am regularly approached by people who introduce themselves as Facebook friends. This is great because however wonderful these sites can be they are ultimately no substitute for 'real' physical interaction. It is one thing to speak through a site messaging service and another to meet face to face. The internet is meant to facilitate real friendship and not be a replacement for it. Having just a few people you can turn to for help, advice or guidance is worth its weight in gold over time.

CREATE A VIRTUAL SANGHA

Sites to check out:

- Blogger – for blogging;

- Facebook – for friendship and connection;

- Flickr – for sharing photographs;

- Flixster – for sharing movie reviews, ratings and clips;

- LinkedIn – for business networking;

- Lulu – for self-publishing;

- MeetUp – for activities and groups in your area;

- MySpace – for sharing music;

- Twitter – for sharing thoughts;

- YouTube – for sharing video clips.

All of these sites can be easily found by searching through Google.

Ask For Feedback …

One of the benefits of having a *Sangha* is that if you are not sure how your gifts and passions fit in the world you can go and ask for feedback. We need feedback because other people can often spot the gifts and talents that we are blind to. We do not always know when or why our work is appreciated. We do not always know why things are working out well or how we can improve our performance. Constructive feedback can help you improvise and grow, learn new skills and identify mistakes so they are avoided in the future.

Constructive feedback tends to be clear, honest and goal oriented. It aims at providing solutions to challenges or problems, and if feedback is done skilfully, then it can also build healthy relationships between colleagues and between managers and employees. Feedback can also be useful when thinking about a new project or business venture. In 1998, three college friends had the idea of creating natural fruit smoothies. They had developed a few recipes, but were nervous about giving up their regular jobs. They decided to set up a stall at a small music festival in London, and put up a sign saying 'Do you think we should give up our day jobs to make these smoothies?' They put out a bin with a sign saying 'Yes' and another bin with a sign saying 'No', and asked customers to use the empty bottles to vote. At the end of the festival the 'Yes' bin was full, so they resigned their jobs. Innocent Drinks is a company that currently has over 70 per cent of the UK smoothie market, worth just under £170 million.

EXERCISE

Ask for Feedback

Mostly we do not know our qualities, skills and strengths, and this is why it is important to ask other people for their feedback.

- Ask your partner/spouse for feedback on your personal qualities, skills and strengths.
- Ask three close friends for feedback on your personal qualities, skills and strengths.
- Ask three work colleagues for feedback on your personal qualities, skills and strengths.

Declaration of Intention

1. I am ready to witness and transform all suffering arising from my work. I am ready to release all limiting conditioning, beliefs, assumptions, unconscious agreements, obligations, drama, persecuting, rescuing and victim consciousness that appear to block me.

2. I am ready to be more authentic, present, conscious and aware in my life and work. I am ready to release any excessive reliance on living on autopilot. I am ready to be 100 per cent courageously myself.

3. I am ready to transform my attitude and perspective in my work. I am ready to face all my fears about the present and the future. I am ready to see a bright, expansive, inviting, hopeful future opening before me.

4. I am ready to acknowledge that my time on earth is limited. I am ready to acknowledge that my time is precious. I am ready to use my time more wisely.

5. I am ready to embrace the fullness of my gifts, resources, strengths and talents. I am ready to use my intellect with my imagination and intuition. I am ready to play to my strengths. I am ready to find my niche in the world. I am ready to listen to feedback and use it wisely.

6. I am ready for fun, humour, laughter and creative play in my work. I am ready to take myself lightly.

7. I am ready for fun, playful, supportive people to enter my life. I am ready to reach out and connect meaningfully with other explorers and pioneers in my chosen fields.

8. I am ready for my work to be a love affair. I am ready to know my heartfelt values. I am ready for enthusiasm and joy to enter into my work. I am ready to love the work I do. I am ready for my life's work to be revealed to me. I am ready to dream my work into being.

9. I am ready to flow like water rather than struggle. I am ready to take effortless action in alignment with my heartfelt values. I am ready to be in the right place at the right time. I am ready for my work to unfold with ease and grace. I am ready to work with ever more bliss.

10. I am ready to take this journey and find my own way. I am ready to trust in my inner guidance and see this journey through, wherever that shall lead me.

Chapter 8

Use Your Intuition

Your work is to discover your work and then with
all your heart to give yourself to it.

The Buddha

. . . .

The film *Revolutionary Road* was about a working couple in the mid-1950s. Frank Wheeler (Leonardo DiCaprio) and April Wheeler (Kate Winslet) are in the seventh year of their marriage. They have a life that appears on the surface to be perfect. They live in the Connecticut suburbs with their two young children. Frank commutes daily to New York City where he works in an office job, April stays at home and works as a housewife. But below the idyllic surface they are not happy. April has sacrificed her dream and Frank hates the work he does.

Be Whole-Brained …

Being whole-brained is the way we are basically designed. This is not the way we are taught to use our brain. When we use all of our brain, more of our resourcefulness becomes available to us. However, since we are taught to be more left-brained, we are kept in a state of lopsidedness and this will, to some degree, limit us and prevent us from fully flowing into a new paradigm of work.

We have an amazing gift, our brain with a neocortex made up of two halves, a left hemisphere and a right hemisphere. The two parts are connected to each other by a thick cable of nerves at the base of each side. Experimentation has shown that these different hemispheres of the brain are responsible for different kinds of thinking. The left brain is more logical, sequential, rational, analytical and objective. The right brain is more random, intuitive, holistic, subjective and synthesizing. It looks at the whole picture rather than detail. The left brain gives us the ability to be practical, create strategies, focus, plan, analyse, structure, understand and design. The right brain gives us the ability to imagine, dream, fantasize, dare, feel and intuit.

If the rational mind is the analyser, the intuitive mind is the synthesizer. It creates the big picture out of all the small details. It opens us to that sudden flash of insight that makes everything crystal clear. When we can analyse *and* synthesize, we are whole-brain thinkers. Most of the great geniuses of history were whole-brain thinkers. For instance, the artist Pablo Picasso worked in a right-brain field yet demonstrated great left-brain thinking in his many notes about the specific combinations of colours he used in his art. Then we have Albert Einstein, a wonderful whole-brain thinker who created his theory of relativity out of a daydream. Lewis Carroll, author of *Alice in Wonderland*, was a deacon in holy orders and a university lecturer. Perhaps the greatest known whole-brain thinker is Leonardo da Vinci, who was an artist painter – he painted the *Mona Lisa* and *The Last Supper* – and also a scientist and engineer. His studies include an enormous range of interests and preoccupations, from compositions for paintings, studies of faces and emotions, to architecture, machines and helicopters.

Nowadays it is rarer to find a whole-brain thinker, because we are taught to be left-brained. We are educated this way because so much employment over the last couple of hundred years or so has been ideally suited for left-brain-dominant people. Jobs such as administration, engineering, IT, law, medicine, project managing and teaching rely heavily on left-brain detail planning and calculation. Most importantly, they also tend to pay much better than right-brain creative jobs such as acting, singing, playing music and writing – except for the very top 1 per cent.

The Industrial Age helped to shape the modern education system. For years, education has been about learning information by rote, sitting tests, and the teacher being the dispenser of knowledge. With the virtual revolution the education system has been forced to adapt and become more student-centred. Even so, it is still about developing the logical left brain. This is not ideal, as we are really only using half our brain. For instance, a left-brain software engineer can design a website, but the end result will not look very creative. A left-brain manager can come up with a vision for a company, but the end result will not be very inspirational. A left-brain architect will be able to design a very functional building, perhaps building on designs that have gone before, but the end result will lack real imagination or innovation.

Of course, the idea is not just to be right-brained. A few manage to resist the indoctrination of the education system by rebelling and going the other way. The trouble is, though, that if you are right-brain dominant with little development of the left brain, then you are at best a creative, imaginative dreamer, and at worst a fantasist. In either case, there may be lots of ideas, but not much practically happening. We need both sides of the brain; to be a whole person with both sides working together synergistically.

Right-Brain Intuition ...

There are tremendous treasures in the right brain – treasures such as creativity, imagination and intuition. The Oxford Dictionary defines *intuition* as 'the ability to understand or know something immediately, without conscious reasoning'. It is derived from a Latin word meaning 'to see within'. Intuition is a skill that has been much valued for thousands of years.

Seers and psychics have existed since the beginning of time, using their powers of intuition to help others. From the biblical visionary Joseph who interpreted dreams for the Egyptian pharaoh, to the priestesses of Delphi in ancient Greece who spoke the will of the gods, to modern-day shamanic bone throwers, card readers and well-known mystics such as Edgar Cayce.

For thousands of years, shamans and priestesses used their intuition and psychic abilities to help their communities. Often these abilities meant the difference between life and death. If you were a tribal medicine man or woman and you could not divine the nearest food source for your tribe, then your tribe starved and you were out of a job. If you were a medicine healer and you were unable to heal a patient, then your reputation would suffer, and if this happened too often you would be out of a job.

Although intuition is not so much valued nowadays, it still operates in many different lines of work; most people just do not call it intuition. For instance, most people do not shop rationally. You may know you need a pair of shoes, but when it comes to the purchase it happens on a feeling and not through logic. When the product ticks all the boxes and feels right, then the purchase is made.

Intuition is a feeling, but it is more than that. Your intuition allows you to know information that you cannot acquire by inference or observation, reason or experience. Intuition is your direct way of sensing the truth of your reality. Intuition is able to guide you in ways that your rational mind cannot. It can help you solve problems and make decisions in ways that your

. . . .

April has forgone her dream of becoming an actress, and although Frank
hates his job he does not know what else to do with his life. Then one
day, April has an inspiration and suggests that they move to Paris. She
has worked out that between their savings and selling their house they
will have enough money to live in Paris for six months without working.
This would give Frank the time to explore what he really wants to do
with his life. Frank eventually comes around to the idea and they come
alive and also fall in love again. But events conspire to thwart the dream.
Frank is offered a major promotion and April discovers she is pregnant.
Frank changes his mind about their dream and starts listening to his head
instead of his heart. This will have fatal consequences.

. . . .

rational mind is not designed to do. We are naturally intuitive. Research
at Yale University has shown that the development of intuition in children
begins very early on. They discovered that by six months of age a child is able
to assess someone's intentions towards them and decide whether they are a
likely friend or foe!

What Blocks Your Intuition ...

Mostly we are taught to suppress our intuitive impulses, although it is likely
that people were allowed to be far more intuitive before the Industrial Age.
Living close to the land in supportive communities would encourage this
ability more naturally than working long hours in a factory.

Nowadays, we work fewer hours and have more leisure time, although
this does not necessarily make us more intuitive. With distractions such

as TV, internet, video games, shopping, alcohol and so on, it is hard to be intuitive when our minds are cluttered with tweets, texts and emails. Intuition does not operate through busyness, but through relaxation and inner stillness. The mind needs to be clear, like a still mountain lake, for intuition to work. It is hard to be intuitive when the mind is bombarded with so much bad news in the media. If you want to know how to be more intuitive, one way is to switch off the TV and reduce and filter the information coming into your brain. There is a very wise saying: 'Garbage in, garbage out'. Let the wise take heed!

Beyond being too busy or distracted to develop our intuition, we just do not know what it is or how to go about developing it. We are taught to distrust it. This distrust is highlighted by the film *Revolutionary Road*. We could say that April plays the part of the intuitive mind and Frank the part of the rational mind. Frank as the rational mind got scared by the ideas of the intuitive mind and blocked it. This led to an emotional suppression and shutdown within the marriage. This is how many people relate to intuition, both on the inside and outside. Albert Einstein said, 'The intuitive mind is a sacred gift and the rational mind is a faithful servant. We have created a society that honours the servant and has forgotten the gift.'

Part of what Frank Wheeler was up against was that this was a time of fixed gender roles. This was a time when sexist stereotypes prevailed, such as men are always rational and women are always feeling and irrational. This myth has been culturally reinforced for centuries as, traditionally, women occupied roles that were about nurturing and relating. These roles require empathy, creativity and feeling. The traditional roles of men have demanded different skills and abilities. Although culturally trained to be less reliant on intuition, they have found their own way to access it. Men access intuition through physical activity, sport, military combat and business arenas. To highlight this, there was an interesting experiment conducted by Marine Corps Lieutenant General Paul Van Riper. The General brought his Marines to the New York Mercantile Exchange in 1995, because the jostling, confusing pits reminded him of war rooms during combat. To no one's surprise, the Marines did not fare as well as the traders. But when the situation was reversed and the General brought the traders to the Marines' base to play war games, he was amazed when the traders beat the Marines at war! The traders were better 'gut thinkers', and more thoroughly practised at quickly evaluating risks and acting decisively on imperfect and contradictory information. Interestingly enough, the Corp's official doctrine reads, 'The intuitive approach is more appropriate for ... decisions made in the fluid, rapidly changing conditions of war when time and uncertainty are critical factors, and creativity is a desirable trait.' Well, there you go!

We will feel blocked in using our right-brain intuition if the environment does not support it. In sport there is a certain amount of leeway for intuition, but in many working environments there is not. If you are a right-brain person working in a left-brain job, you will struggle. I have met many people who are doing work that really does not suit their natural temperament. For instance, Jane 'fell into journalism' when she left school. She did so because her mother thought it might be 'fun and stimulating'. She got the job – and it turned her life upside down. Being an intuitive, feeling, right-brained farmer's daughter, she found herself in a cerebral, political, left-brained, urban world – 'everything I was not'. For Jane it was an education, but not one that she necessarily wanted. After qualifying as a senior journalist, she decided to go to university and embarked on a psychology degree – and came out of it with 'a sense of something missing'. Learning about rat-running experiments had not answered her deeper metaphysical questions about life. She had learnt a mixture of Freudian, cognitive, behavioural and humanistic psychology, yet her real interest was for the transpersonal. Her journey led her into the world of investigating health, healing, human potential and consciousness through various jobs. This included working with a scientist investigating the sixth sense; managing a Jungian training institute and undertaking public relations for a natural health centre. She also later trained in a powerful energy psychology which gave her the link she was looking for between the mind, body and spirit and how to work with all three practically. Jane told me, 'It's not been an easy journey, but it's one that is bringing me home to myself at a much deeper level than following any regular career path could have done.'

A big block for some people is that they have little awareness of their personal selves and cannot tell the difference between intuition and inner chatter. There is so much fear being pumped out through the media that this can be internalized and presented as intuition. When we cannot tell the difference between fear and intuition, it becomes unreliable. If we follow the voice of fear, yet believe that our intuition is guiding us, the result will be anything from poor to disastrous. Our intuition gets entwined with the voice of fear when we have fearful beliefs about the world. When we believe that the world is unsafe and that we are not secure, we will seek to use our intuition to stay safe. This is a poor use of our intuition. Even if it works it will only serve to make us paranoid. I knew a very intuitive woman

THE DIFFERENCE BETWEEN FEAR AND INTUITION

The voice of fear wants to keep you safe, the voice of your intuition wants you to stretch and grow. Your intuition may tell you to be cautious in certain circumstances, but it will never incite you to be afraid. Your intuition seeks to move you towards a desired outcome, even if it guides you in a random way to get there. Your intuition will have a calming and reassuring affect. When you follow your intuition it naturally gets stronger.

who was the head of an organization that taught psychic development and intuition classes. Unfortunately, she was a rather fearful person and used her intuition to spot people she 'knew' she could not trust. This created an atmosphere of distrust and conflict around her. Unlike the voice of fear, our intuition is heart centred, and following its guidance will lead you to feel more empowered, joyful, inspired and uplifted. The voice of fear tells you to find a job that will make you rich, whereas intuition tells you to find a job that you love. The voice of fear tells you to go network and find some people who can be useful to you, whereas intuition tells you to go network and find people you would love to collaborate with.

Intuition Works as Hunches …

Malcolm Gladwell writes in his book *Blink – The Power of Thinking Without Thinking* about an ancient Greek marble statue purchased by the Getty Museum in California in 1983. It was what is known as a kouros – a sculpture of a nude male youth standing with his left leg forwards and his arms at his sides. There are only about 200 in existence, and most have been recovered damaged or in fragments. Before purchasing the piece for $10 million, the museum ran a number of scientific tests, all of which confirmed it to be genuine. However, the piece was a clever fake. Frederico Zert, an art historian, was the first to notice that something wasn't right, although he could not put his finger on why. Evelyn Harrison, a leading expert on Greek sculpture, also had a hunch something was wrong. Thomas Hoving, the former director of the New York Metropolitan Museum of Art, remembered that the word 'fresh' leapt to mind the first time he saw the piece. Each of these experts felt intuitively that something was not right, based on only the small amount of information available to them on first seeing the sculpture. Gladwell calls this 'thin-slicing', the art of reaching 'useable conclusions' based on 'limited information'. Just another way of saying using intuition!

According to Gay Hendricks and Kate Ludeman, authors of *How to Be a Corporate Mystic*, most successful business people are highly intuitive and many follow non-dogmatic forms of spirituality. Just as well intuition is still alive in the workplace, since Daniel H Pink, author of *A Whole New Mind*, says:

> A funny thing happened while we were pressing our noses to the grindstone: The world changed. The future no longer belongs to people who can reason with computer-like logic, speed, and precision. It belongs to a different kind of person with a different kind of mind. Today – amid the uncertainties of an economy that has gone from boom to bust to blah – there's a metaphor that explains what's going on. And it's right inside our heads. In a world upended by outsourcing, deluged with data, and choked with choices, the abilities that matter most are now closer in spirit to the specialties of the right hemisphere – artistry, empathy, seeing the big picture, and pursuing the transcendent.

As Daniel says, many jobs are being lost in the developed West through outsourcing to the developing East. Many relatively cheap knowledge workers are coming online in the East, and many jobs are being lost – mainly left-brain jobs such as computer programming, accounting, legal research and financial analysis. These jobs are migrating across the oceans where they can be done more cheaply. In the current economic climate we need to nurture different talents. Being more left brained just will not do it any more.

In this changeable world, intuition is vital. Intuition can help you in your life and career to make decisions without having all the facts, and it can help you when the way ahead is unclear. Intuition can show you the right way to proceed; it can help you solve problems more easily, find opportunities, connect with the right people, take the right action at the right time and ultimately find or create the work you love. I'm sure you will agree these are pretty strong reasons for taking intuition more seriously. Our intuition operates on many different levels. These levels are not completely separate; they all tend to inter-relate and work synergistically together, just like an orange is one piece of fruit made up of many parts: the skin, the juice, the core, and so on.

Physical

This is the intuition which comes through a 'gut feeling', a physical sensation, a shiver down the spine, butterflies in the stomach, or a feeling of lightness or heaviness. This is where we smell danger before we can see it. Have you ever entered a room and felt uplifted or deflated for no reason? Rupert Sheldrake, a biologist and author of ten books, has also studied intuition. In his book *The Sense of Being Stared At*, he researches how we instinctively know when we are being stared at, even if we cannot see the person staring at us. This skill would have meant the difference between life and death to our nomadic hunter ancestors. This is physical intuition.

Emotional

This is a first impression of 'like or dislike' – feeling a vibe about a person. Have you ever felt intuitively the need to avoid getting involved in certain situations or with certain individuals? Have you ever met a stranger and felt at ease because the vibe was somehow right? This is emotional intuition.

Mental

This is an inspiration, a flash of insight, a thought from nowhere, a solution to a problem, the answer to a question. Have you ever thought of someone and then they phone you soon after? Mental intuition comes via the visual or auditory channels – as images or words inside the mind. This is also the realm of precognition through dreams. Artists, authors, inventors, mathematicians and scientists have been able to access this level of intuition.

Spiritual

This is a transcendental form of intuition. The philosopher Spinoza thought that intuition united the mind with higher consciousness that revealed the underlying order of the Universe. The Buddha under the Bodhi tree received the Four Noble Truths through spiritual insight. This form of intuition reveals insight and spiritual truth; it is accessed by spiritual seekers, shamans and mystics.

Intuition Through the Body ...

We have different levels of intuition and the best place to start to open is with the physical. Most intuitions come first as physical feelings. These feelings can help the other levels to open also. Because of this it is important for you to get out of an intellectualized attitude and into a more gut-orientated approach. Often your intuition will not speak to you first through your imagination or thoughts, at least not in the early stages of awakening; it comes through sensations in your body. You may get a certain gut feeling or a sense of expansiveness in your chest, you may feel lighter or more excited when your intuition is speaking to you. The trouble is, if you are not connected to your body, then you will have no way of connecting with this level of your intuition. So perhaps it's time to get out of your head and into your body!

Intuition, Intention and Imagination ...

Once you have started to practise using your intuition, you can start to engage it in useful ways. But before you get going you need to engage it with a clear idea of what you want. This can be making a choice between different options, problem solving, or a specific goal. You can use it to direct your career, but asking your intuition to help you move towards a new job without any idea of what you want or are looking for is not giving your intuition much

EXERCISE

Get Into Your Body

1. **Relaxation**. Relaxation is an important beginning stage to connecting with your intuition. Do some simple exercise to help you relax such as yoga or tai chi.

2. **Breath**. Become aware of the breath. As you breathe, become aware of places of tension and ease in the body.

3. **Feelings**. Practise staying connected to yourself. Notice the different feelings you have throughout the day. Feelings arise in different parts of the body. Notice where in your body you have these feeling-sensations.

4. **Senses**. Start to notice all the senses, but particularly your sense of touch. Practise touching different things – fabrics, objects – and notice how they feel to the touch. Notice sensations that feel pleasant and unpleasant.

5. **Decision**. If you have a decision to make, such as whether to take action, whether to wait, or whether to go left or go right, tune into each choice for a few minutes and notice how your body reacts to each choice. Notice if you feel expansive or restricted, heavy or light, warm or cold in response to each choice.

to go on. You do not need to know the form of this work, but it is helpful to know the essence. Knowing that you want more creativity or freedom or self-autonomy is giving your intuition direction.

Anne organizes and designs bespoke wedding ceremonies. Her work ranges from large formal religious events to smaller, more intimate family occasions. Part of her work involves organizing and part-writing the ceremony. She has a clear focus for her intuition to work with. She told me, 'I rely on my intuition to inform what I write. The more I trust my intuition, the better the results usually. But I have to be clear at the outset what I am aiming for. The whole process from the start is one of trust. I need to stand back and not allow my "performance" considerations to get in the way. It always comes down to preparation and intention. When they are in place, I sit down and the words pour from me in no time, I know not from where. It is as if "I" am not writing them. I feel blessed to do this work. I know it is no small commitment to choose to commit to love another person for the rest of our lives.'

Your intuition is like a dog that wants to fetch a stick. It needs direction, it needs a stick. Linda grew up with a strange passion – she loved crime. Although this was an unusual passion, her father encouraged her to follow her heart. So she went to university and gained a criminology degree. Then she entered the job market. Using both her intuition and reasoning mind she found some interesting jobs. She also turned down some interesting jobs. What she was looking for was work that would feed her passion. For example, she was once asked if she wanted to work in the fraud department of a large clearing bank. Although the job was well paid she tuned in and declined – she felt that the work would not be 'juicy' enough.

Intuition can be of help in all sorts of ways, not only in searching for work. It can also be helpful in progressing projects. For a year or more, I knew I wanted to write another book, but was not really sure exactly what I wanted to write about. Then in January 2010 I had a dream that gave me the subject and the title and what it was generally about! I leapt out of bed and started on the book that morning. And voilà, here is the finished product!

Intuition has many practical applications. For instance, the amazing Findhorn Foundation near Inverness in Scotland was built on intuition. It all started when Peter and Eileen Caddy and Dorothy Maclean came to north-east Scotland in 1957 to manage the Cluny Hill Hotel in the town of Forres. This they did remarkably successfully with a lot of help from Eileen, who received guidance in her meditations from an inner divine source she called 'the still small voice within'. Peter ran the hotel following Eileen's guidance. In this unorthodox way, Cluny Hill swiftly became a thriving and successful four-star hotel. After several years, however, Peter and Eileen's employment was terminated, and with nowhere to go and little money, they moved with their three young sons and Dorothy to a caravan in the nearby seaside village of Findhorn. Feeding so many people on unemployment benefit was not easy, so Peter decided to start growing vegetables. The land in the caravan park was sandy and dry, but he persevered. Dorothy started to receive specific guidance on how to make the most of their garden. Following this guidance – despite the barren sandy soil of the Findhorn Bay Caravan Park – they grew huge plants, herbs and flowers of dozens of kinds. Word spread, horticultural experts came and were stunned, and the garden at Findhorn became famous.

As you can see, intuition has many practical applications, from creating a successful business to building a successful garden to finding solutions to day-to-day problems. The conscious mind can work out problems, but there are times when it is best left to the intuition. This is often true when the problem is complex and beyond the reasoning abilities of the conscious mind. On one occasion, Jenny had a seemingly very difficult problem to solve at work involving staff rotas. Not being very mathematical, her conscious mind was getting tired of thinking about the problem – there seemed to be so many factors involved. She decided to hand it over to her intuition and just sleep on it. To her surprise she awoke in the morning with the clear answer. She quickly wrote it down before she forgot, and that morning started to scope it out and see if it really was a good solution. The solution seemed to work and it was soon implemented and it did work. Although she left this job many years ago, the last she heard was that the same rota system was still being used.

EXERCISE 1

Trust Your First Impressions

- Pay attention to your first impressions when going somewhere for the first time, meeting a new person or thinking about different options, and write them down.

- Exercise your hunch-making abilities by guessing what will happen in the next scene in a movie, who will call you today, what a friend will say to you next, who will win the game, and so on.

- Write down a question and then write down the first answer that pops into your head. Put the paper aside for a day or so, and look at your answers again.

- Ask for guidance and be open to the answer coming through dreams, or through chance conversation.

- Don't try to 'force' your intuition, just trust that it will come. Learn to recognize the 'aha' moment, when your intuition is speaking with you.

EXERCISE 2

Intuition and New Possibilities

In this exercise you are going to use both sides of the brain to come up with new possibilities in your work. You will need to play this game with at least one other person; however, two other people would be ideal.

1. On an A3 sheet of paper draw three circles that interlink – known as a Venn diagram. In one circle write 'dreams', in another 'passions', in the other 'values'. Then spend 20 minutes writing down as many things as possible in each circle that relate to the category.

2. Now randomly pick one item from each of the circles and put them together, so you now have one dream, one passion and one value.

3. Now it is the turn of the other two players. The game is for them to come up with as many possible jobs that would fit a person with this dream, this passion and this value. Encourage them to be practical, imaginative and outrageous. Above all, have fun.

4. Review your list of possible jobs. How attractive are they? How completely random are they? Would you consider doing any of them? If not, why not? List your reasons.

5. Now it is the next person's turn.

EXERCISE 3

Intuition and Problem Solving

1. **Define**. Define the problem to be solved and the outcome you would like. The more specific you can be the better.

2. **Gather**. Use your rational mind to gather all the pieces of the jigsaw, all the relevant pieces of information. However, do not try to use your rational mind to find the answer.

3. **Play**. Play with all the pieces of the puzzle, and get a feel for the puzzle to be solved. This is not about solving but playing. Just get a feel for all the aspects involved.

4. **Open**. This part involves trusting your intuition to deliver the answer. Expect an answer. To do this, just let go of all the pieces and allow your intuition to deliver the messages to you. It may come internally through an idea or dream, or it might come externally through a book or conversation that points the way. Remember the messages may be metaphoric or literal.

5. **Revisit**. Keep revisiting the problem for short periods from time to time to keep your intuition engaged until the answer comes. This process might end quickly or take a little time, depending on the nature and complexity of the problem.

Declaration of Intention

1. I am ready to witness and transform all suffering arising from my work. I am ready to release all limiting conditioning, beliefs, assumptions, unconscious agreements, obligations, drama, persecuting, rescuing and victim consciousness that appear to block me.

2. I am ready to be more authentic, present, conscious and aware in my life and work. I am ready to release any excessive reliance on living on autopilot. I am ready to be 100 per cent courageously myself.

3. I am ready to transform my attitude and perspective in my work. I am ready to face all my fears about the present and the future. I am ready to see a bright, expansive, inviting, hopeful future opening before me.

4. I am ready to acknowledge that my time on earth is limited. I am ready to acknowledge that my time is precious. I am ready to use my time more wisely.

5. I am ready to embrace the fullness of my gifts, resources, strengths and talents. I am ready to use my intellect with my imagination and intuition. I am ready to play to my strengths. I am ready to find my niche in the world. I am ready to listen to feedback and use it wisely.

6. I am ready for fun, humour, laughter and creative play in my work. I am ready to take myself lightly.

7. I am ready for fun, playful, supportive people to enter my life. I am ready to reach out and connect meaningfully with other explorers and pioneers in my chosen fields.

8. I am ready for my work to be a love affair. I am ready to know my heartfelt values. I am ready for enthusiasm and joy to enter into my work. I am ready to love the work I do. I am ready for my life's work to be revealed to me. I am ready to dream my work into being.

9. I am ready to flow like water rather than struggle. I am ready to take effortless action in alignment with my heartfelt values. I am ready to be in the right place at the right time. I am ready for my work to unfold with ease and grace. I am ready to work with ever more bliss.

10. I am ready to take this journey and find my own way. I am ready to trust in my inner guidance and see this journey through, wherever that shall lead me.

Chapter 9

Work and Play

What work I have done I have done because it has been play. If it had been work I shouldn't have done it.

Mark Twain

· ·

In 1957 a Buddha statue had to be relocated from a temple in Thailand because of a new highway being constructed through Bangkok. When the crane began to lift the giant idol, it was so heavy that it began to crack. Since it was raining, the head monk was concerned about damaging the statue and asked that it be lowered back to the ground and covered with a large canvas to protect it from the rain. Later that evening, the head monk went to check on the statue. He shone his flashlight under the canvas and noticed a strange reflection. He went to fetch a chisel and hammer from the monastery and began to chip away at the clay. After many hours of labour the head monk stood face to face with a solid-gold ten-and-a-half-foot tall Buddha. Historians believe that several hundred years before, the statue was camouflaged to protect it from the invading Burmese army. The secret of the statue had been forgotten for centuries.

The Dangers of Conformity and Seriousness ...

Work is one way we can train ourselves in the twin dangers of conformity and seriousness. This is the hard clay that is poured over our innate sense of lightness, creativity, fun and desire to enjoy life. Our golden authentic selves can be smothered with conformity and seriousness. In time we may forget that life and work can be enjoyable. We may learn that work is no laughing matter. This is a heads-down-and-get-on-with-work approach. Not much fun at all.

Seriousness was much valued in the Industrial Age, where conformity was needed to keep the machines going. Seriousness is a disease of the outgoing age of work. You can tell if you are suffering from the disease of seriousness by answering just a few simple questions. Do you ever feel you need to justify your salary? Does you workplace have a 'never mix business with pleasure' attitude? Do you ever feel that it is wrong to be light-hearted at work? Is your work ever fun? If the answer to all these questions is 'no', then you probably have some lightening up to do. It is not that your work is to blame; at some level you have bought into the idea that work is serious. And this is a very serious idea. You see seriousness leads to hard work and in this current age of work this will not get you very far at all.

Now work is evolving, it is more about cooperation, creativity, innovation and play. Yes, play! Most successful people now think of themselves as players, not workers. This is a very different approach to work. And it is not just a quaint idea – most good companies realize that nowadays it's not just money that keeps people at work. More and more, companies are being pushed to offer conditions and contexts that support people overall: not just on the job, but in areas of personal wellness and quality of life. Most companies realize that they cannot afford to be overly serious. Where a company is too serious, the motivation of staff will tend to suffer and plummet. Research shows that motivated employees tend to be productive employees.

Don't worry, your boss is not going to start telling bad jokes to keep motivation high. It is more subtle than that! We are in an age of work that does not just allow for play, it encourages and celebrates it. For instance, take the innovative site YouTube, created in 2005: it gives global access to an unlimited show reel of amateur singers, dancers, performers, comedians and practically anything you can think of. It is not just YouTube that celebrates play and uniqueness. On many sites such as Facebook, being normal is the equivalent of being dull and boring, and therefore invisible.

A friend of mine started working for a company called Happy Computers. She told me that it was a really fun place to work. I did some research and found that Happy Computers believe that people are basically resourceful, which is no bad place to start. They state that 'all people (with no exceptions) are born with enormous intelligence and tremendous eagerness to learn'. I dug a little deeper and found that the company is based on some interesting principles, including: trust your staff; make your staff feel good; give freedom with clear guidelines; be open and transparent; recruit for attitude, train for skill; celebrate mistakes; and create a community of mutual benefit. What a great ethos for treating your staff. I also discovered that they believe that learning should be fun. I was intrigued and went along for some software training. The premises were not like any corporate venue I had ever visited. The lounge area was very colourful and relaxing. I was put at ease immediately, and I enjoyed the training. I discovered for myself that fun is also effective. They work to the old adage 'Tell me and I will forget; show me and I will remember; involve me and I will understand.' At the annual Institute of IT Training awards in 2009, Happy Computers was named as the very best provider of IT training in the UK. Happy had won Silver in 2006, 2007 and 2008.

While researching Happy Computers I also came across another pioneering organization called Great Place to Work Institute, which has been assisting companies across the world since 1998 to make changes to their workplace culture and environment, with the overall goal of creating a better society of happier workers. They gather information and ideas from their connections with some of the best companies around the world to promote how to create great places to work. Great Place to Work Institute says, 'Firms that have managed to maintain trust, loyalty and engagement may have the competitive edge in the new business climate.'

It is not just companies that are pioneering happiness, there are also pioneering individuals who have learnt to be successful through play and fun. Take Richard Branson – he says about himself that he never went into business to make money. Yet he found that when he has the most fun, then money just seems to come. Being dyslexic, he struggled with the left-brain school system of the 1960s. However, his creative talents eventually surfaced during his adolescent school years, and he became involved in student activism. He had the interesting idea of starting a student newspaper that focused on students rather than the schools. Somehow, Branson persuaded Peter Blake, who designed the Beatles' *Sergeant Pepper* album cover, to donate some artwork and give an interview to the student newspaper. After the successful launch of the paper, his school headmaster wrote: 'Congratulations, Branson. I predict that you will either go to prison or become a millionaire.'

Apprentice Yourself to Play …

As children we knew how to play. We climbed trees, ran around the local park, listened to stories, made things out of Lego and played with dolls. This is how we took our initial steps towards an enduring sense of self, creativity, resilience, resourcefulness and freedom. Play is how we first learn to take control of our own time. Some educational approaches realize the importance of play, such as the amazing 40-year experiment in progressive schooling in Central Italy known as the Reggio Emilia Approach. The motto of this schooling method is to do 'nothing without joy'. Unfortunately, most schools are not that progressive, so our playful creative sides get covered over with the hard clay of conformity and seriousness. Then play has no place in our world any more. Then we are in trouble and need help.

Fortunately, not everyone gets covered in hard clay. A few brave individuals join the resistance and promote non-conformity and creative play. These people are often called eccentrics. The word 'eccentric' derives from the Greek word *ekkentros*, meaning 'out of the centre'. Thus the word is not about acting strangely, but about being more yourself. Eccentricity is often associated with genius, intellectual giftedness and creativity. Eccentric behaviour can appear odd and illogical on the outside, but it is merely a reflection of the individual's original mind.

In our conformist society, eccentrics are the ones that pioneer the way into non-conformity, innovation and originality. One of my favourite eccentrics was the great Oscar Wilde. He lived in a time of moral conservatism in Victorian England, yet loved to wear flamboyant clothes. Whilst studying at Oxford University his room was decorated with bright blue china, sunflowers and peacock feathers. At times he would even walk through the streets of Oxford with a lobster on a leash. I would not choose to live this way, but I do admire Oscar Wilde for his courage to be fiercely himself.

There are many contemporary eccentrics in the world. Take, for instance, the artist Damien Hirst, who created a life-size cast of a human skull in platinum, called *For the Love of God*. This piece was covered entirely by over 8,500 flawless pavé-set diamonds. In the centre of the forehead was a large pink diamond. The skull's name was supposedly inspired by Hirst's mother, who once asked, 'For the love of God, what are you going to do next?'

Eccentrics believe that it is okay to be themselves. This is an invitation to become an apprentice eccentric. You do not have to dress flamboyantly or take pet lobsters out for walks on a leash to be eccentric. You do need to ease into a conversation where you can discover who you are and what you want to do – even if that does go against some social conventions. I once had a coaching client who was a successful portrait artist. The issue was that he was not really doing the work that he loved. What he really wanted to paint were things that other people might find shocking. He called this unrealized urge 'the elephant in the room'. Squashing this urge in him was a conditioned idea that painting had to be perfect. As an apprentice eccentric your job is to clear out the hard clay so that you can play, get creative and have fun doing the things you love to do. And it does not matter if other people do not agree with you – it does matter that what you do feels right for you.

Eccentrics can teach us to be fiercely ourselves and not to take ourselves too seriously. They can teach us to be adventurous, chill out, and open up to more play and fun. Fun is good for your health – having fun helps you to release endorphins into your bloodstream. Play is a right-brain activity; of course, if you want come at play from a more left-brained perspective, you could aim to increase your overall level of joy by 13 per cent in a week's time, and aim for an overall increase of 20 per cent in the next financial quarter. Include an increase in your output of fun in the following week by 17.5 per cent, aiming for an overall increase of 21.5 per cent in the next financial quarter. Only kidding! You could give it a go I suppose. And do let me know if it works!

Play is not just for people in potentially creative jobs such as artists, choreographers or music directors. It is also important in jobs such as nursing, teaching, farming and any other job where play is not normally allowed. The prolific inventor and scientist Thomas Edison, creator of the motion picture camera and the electric light bulb, said, 'I never did a day's work in all my life. It was all fun.' Similarly, if you look around you will find people having fun in all walks of life. A friend of mine met a woman on a train and they started to chat about their work. Apparently this woman's job was to watch films for 40 hours a week, and select the ones to be shown in a chain of independent cinemas in South East England. What an amazing job – the kind of job I would love to have gone into instead of banking!

Fun also can happen in the rather serious world of medicine. I met Patch Adams in the late 1990s. Patch Adams is a medical doctor and a clown. He is also a social activist who has devoted 40 years to changing America's health care system. He believes that laughter, joy and creativity are an integral part of the healing process. He founded The Gesundheit Institute with a group of 20 friends, including 3 doctors, who moved into a 6-bedroom home. They opened a free hospital, which was open 24 hours a day 7 days a week for all manner of medical problems from birth to death. Though staff had to work outside jobs in order to support themselves and their families, no one left for the first nine years. The inspirational work of Patch Adams eventually drew the attention of Hollywood, leading to the blockbuster film of his life starring Robin Williams. To this day, Adams still teaches a prescription for medical care based on humour and play, which he sees as essential to physical and emotional health.

You must have chaos in your soul to give birth to a dancing star.

Friedrich Nietzsche

The Play Ethic …

Buckminster Fuller said, 'You never change things by fighting the existing reality. To change something, build a new model that makes the existing model obsolete.' For centuries, generations have worked in accordance with an old model, the Protestant Work Ethic. Here, 'good' work was based on generally accepted principles of thrift, discipline and hard work. The Victorian Scottish writer Thomas Carlyle said in 1843, 'Labour is life. From the innermost heart of the worker rises his God-given force … in idleness alone is there perpetual despair.' The work ethic is a tough and resilient set of ideas because, as Max Weber said, it lies at the heart of the 'spirit of capitalism'. Now this ethic is dissolving because it no longer represents the spirit of the current age of work.

However, the old-fashioned work ethic is not leaving without a fight. For instance, take Jack, a very bright Cambridge graduate who became a successful entrepreneur at a young age. He graduated with a double first-class degree and in 2004 co-founded a company that brought personal development training and coaching to young people. The company was a great success, not only in that it helped make a difference to a great many people, but also in financial terms. Jack worked hard, but after several years of building the company and achieving the success he wanted, he felt that there was something missing. He felt he needed more time to think, reflect and consider his options. Things came to a head when Jack decided he wanted to spend a month in India with his girlfriend. This was challenging since it went against the company's work ethic. Jack believed in the company, but there was 'a new conversation' brewing inside of him. Interestingly enough, his company was based in a place called The Fun Factory. I would say that there is a big clue there somewhere!

Fortunately for people like Jack, there is a new ethic emerging in the workplace that directly challenges our old thinking about work. Pat Kane, author of *The Play Ethic*, says, 'The play ethic is about having the confidence to be spontaneous, creative and empathic across every area of your life. It is about placing yourself, your passions and enthusiasms at the centre of your life.' Play is not being idle or frivolous, rather it is a state of mind where you are an active creator. Play is the foundation for being creative. When you learn to play you are learning to clear your mental and physical space of stuff that is depressing you. This means you have more inner space for activities that are enjoyable, imaginative and fun.

Brian Sutton-Smith, the Dean of Play Studies at the University of Pennsylvania, says, 'The opposite of play isn't work. It's depression.' Play is not about leisure or slumped relaxation. Quite the opposite, play is dynamic and focused. According to Pat Kane, 'To call yourself a "player", rather than a "worker", is to immediately widen your conception of who you are and what you might be capable of doing. It is to dedicate yourself to realizing your full human potential; to be active, not passive.'

About the same time that I first came across the play ethic I also came across a couple of true stories about play. The first was about a man who fought in the First World War. He had been a soldier in the field artillery. In those days they used horses to pull the gun carriages. After the manoeuvres they would sometimes unhitch the horses and use them to play polo. During those games he felt an exhilaration he had never felt before or after. He assumed that only playing polo would make him feel so good. Then, in his 80s, he read a book that encouraged him to play more in his life. He realized that the feelings he had in his youth were not necessarily about polo. And so he started some new activities: he listened to music, he learned how to work in a garden, and he tried other things that restored to him the exhilaration of his youth. He discovered you are never too old to start to play.

The second story was about a man called Paul in the early 1960s who started a new job in a factory in the north of England. He started sweeping the factory yard, then he was moved onto the shop floor. However, his real passion was for music and he was in a band. Then one day a couple of mates from the band showed up at the factory and said they had a gig at a local club. Paul told them that he could not go because he had a steady job 'that pays £7 and 14 shillings a week'. But later he thought better of it, 'bunked' over the factory wall and went to play at the gig. Paul McCartney later said of this: 'Pretty shrewd move really, as things turned out.'

> *Play's ultimate function ... is to maintain our adaptability, vigour and optimism in the face of an uncertain, risky and demanding world.*
>
> **Pat Kane**

WHY IS PLAY IMPORTANT?

- Play allows for time to be still and idle.
- Play helps us relax and let go.
- Play is an important way to learn.
- Play connects and bonds us to others.
- Play allows for trust and intimacy.
- Play teaches perseverance.
- Play stimulates the imagination.
- Play opens up empathic abilities.
- Play helps to release locked thoughts in the head.
- Play engages the whole-brain.
- Play helps us stay absorbed and present in what we do.
- Play allows for sharper memory and focus.
- Play allows for creative ideas to flow.
- Play allows us to explore new ideas and ways of doing things.
- Play helps us be more productive.
- Playful working environments retain talented people.
- Play is the perfect antidote for a busy life.
- Play revitalizes the human spirit.

Play Without Agenda …

Bernie DeKoven, one of the originators of the New Games Movement, has devoted his life to developing games that bring people together in the context of playing for fun. Bernie says, 'When the fun gets deep enough it can heal the world.' Bernie believes it is okay to lose. 'Getting beaten, fair and square, by your own grandkid, is one of life's great events.' He also says that nobody has to lose. For some reason we create competitive games that we take far too seriously. How often have you seen a child cry because they 'lost' at something? Competition separates, rather than unites. Even if you try to keep the competition friendly and fun, the very existence of winners and losers shifts the focus of the game away from fun and playfulness. Of course, it is possible to play a competitive game and still retain a sense of fun. But it is challenging, and you only have to look at competitive sports where there is big money involved to see that a game can turn into something more aggressive. In the games you play, how about playing just for fun, playing to learn how you and other people tick, or playing to find real emotional intimacy and connection with other people?

I asked Yumicho, a play therapist, about her work. She works with children from deprived backgrounds to help them connect with their creative, authentic, spontaneous nature. Play is a powerful tool to help children transform themselves when they cannot change their external circumstances. She told me that adults often find it hard to play – they are more resistant than children because they associate play with a loss of control. Play is very powerful tool that can help us to transform stress, to know our true gifts and also our true purpose in life. Yumicho says that deep down we all know how to play, even when we have been conditioned to forget.

I like to hang out with creative and playful people. One good friend who has taught me lots about play is Lisa. Everything Lisa does in life has a playful edge. She trained and worked as a teacher in the United States, but eventually took some time out to live in the south of Ireland to explore

EXERCISE 1

Play Time

- Allow daily time for creative play. Explore both structured and unstructured play time.
- Ask yourself a number of open-ended questions around play and fun.
- What kind of activities would you love to do, are you intrigued to do, or might you like to try out?
- Explore different avenues of play such as painting, board games, storytelling, tree climbing, or charades. How about organizing a treasure hunt, a camping trip, a play, body painting, or a star-gazing outing?

EXERCISE 2

Create a Fun Project

- Decide on something that you would like to create as a fun project. Make it something that includes elements of play and has a tangible end result.
- The project could be something creative that you do by yourself, such as cooking or writing an article, story or piece of poetry. It could be something like creating a short video clip or series of clips. Or it could be a project involving other people, such as setting up a raw chocolate-making group, a meditation group or a film club.
- Dedicate a set amount of time to this project, perhaps on the same day or time each week. This is important to create a strong boundary around the project.
- Record your ideas and progress. Follow through until the project is done. Share the results of the project with others.

the country, discover herself, take some personal development courses and have an adventure. I asked her about her work and she replied, 'My job is whatever I'm doing in this moment. A couple of hours ago I was fanning the inner flames of gratitude and bliss on a clifftop overlooking the Atlantic. This morning, I did some visualization work for people I love, and that was my work. Tomorrow, I will be training clients in the gym, and that will be my work.'

And will you succeed? Yes indeed, yes indeed!

Ninety-eight and three-quarters percent guaranteed.

Dr Seuss

Play and Laughter ...

In the mid 1960s Norman Cousins – author, editor, political journalist and peace advocate – flew home from a trip abroad with a mild fever. Within a week he could hardly move and soon he was soon diagnosed with a chronic and degenerative condition. Doctors said he would be in a wheelchair within a few months to a year. Cousins believed his condition was due to the tremendous pressure he had been under at work. Cousins checked out, concluding that hospital, with its culture of overmedication and general negativity, was 'no place for a person who is seriously ill'. He stopped taking all medication and instead took large doses of Vitamin C. Then he booked into a hotel and brought in a movie projector and a large supply of funny films, including many Candid Camera tapes and several Marx Brothers movies. On his first night Cousins found that he laughed so hard he was able to have several hours of pain-free sleep. When the pain returned he would simply turn the projector back on and the laughter would re-induce sleep. Within days he was feeling much better, and within a few months he was back at work with almost perfect health.

E X E R C I S E

Humour at Work

- Wear funny socks or underwear to work.
- Find a funny CD or MP3 and play it on your way to work.
- Look for funny things around you such as in advertising, newspapers and magazines.
- Look out for funny things on the way to work.
- Have funny sayings around your desk that lighten you up.
- Have a humour bulletin board.
- Look out for the funny foibles and quirky behaviour of your co-workers.
- Laugh with people rather than at them.
- Smile often for no good reason, smiling is a precursor to laughing.
- Find ways to laugh with your co-workers for no real reason at all.
- Find others with a funny sense of humour and go hang out with them at breaks.
- Add a humour break to meetings.

Humour is definitely good for your health. According to laughter therapist Edna Junkins, 'Laughter is the human gift for coping and for survival.' This is backed up by comedian Bill Cosby who says, 'If you can laugh at it, you can survive it.' Humour is important in the workplace. Michael Kerr, author of *You Can't Be Serious – Putting Humour to Work*, stresses that humour is not only a tool in the workplace, but also a barometer indicating how healthy and well-functioning a workplace is. He says that humour can help us combat stress, and boost morale, creativity and productivity. Nothing works faster or more dependably to bring your mind, body and spirit back into balance than a good laugh. Humour lightens the way, inspires hope, connects you to others and keeps you grounded. Laughter can also help in making us feel better, see things more clearly, and more enthusiastically weigh options. Laughter helps us roll with the punches that inevitably come our way and there is little doubt that in today's stressful world, we need to laugh much more. Laughter is good for you because it relieves physical tension and stress, decreases stress

· ·

There is a story about a middle-aged Jewish woman whose children had long grown up and left home. One day she suddenly decided that she needed to go to the Himalayas to talk with a Buddhist lama. She went to the travel agent who said, 'The Himalayas, are you sure? It's a long trip, they speak a different language, have strange food and the main way to travel is by oxcart. How about London, Paris or Florida instead?' But she was adamant and so the journey was arranged. On the appointed day she set off wearing her best outfit. First she travelled by plane, then by train, then by bus and then finally by oxcart until she arrived at the far-off Buddhist monastery in Nepal. There, a monk told her that the lama she was seeking was meditating in a cave far up the mountain and could not be disturbed. But being a determined woman and having come this far she would not be put off. Finally, the monk relented, saying that she could speak to the lama briefly for only a minute or so. She agreed and set off with some monks and sherpas and climbed the winding steep path to the top of the mountain. With a great effort of will she reached the top and entered the cave in which the lama was meditating. She stood in the narrow entrance of the cave and could just make out the silhouette of the meditating figure. Taking a breath in, she said in a loud clear voice, 'Moshe, enough is enough. It's your mother ... come home already!'

· ·

M E D I T A T I O N

The Inner Smile

From the Taoist tradition of ancient China comes the Inner Smile Meditation. This was taught to enhance health, happiness and longevity.

1. Begin by relaxing. Direct your attention around your body, starting from the head down. Feel yourself in a natural, relaxed, neutral state. Put your attention on your lips and the corners of your mouth. Notice the feeling of the corners of your mouth as they are in their neutral, relaxed state.

2. Then, ever so slightly, raise the corners of the mouth until you feel the 'inner smile'. Mindfully lift the corners of your mouth, ever so mindfully, until you feel a warm sense of well-being.

3. Bring your attention to your heart and imagine that there is an 'inner smile' radiating from your head.

4. Bring your attention to your chest and again imagine that there is an 'inner smile' radiating from your chest – your heart and lungs.

5. Move to the belly and imagine that there is an 'inner smile' radiating from your belly – your liver, spleen, stomach and intestinal tract.

6. Move to the pelvis area and imagine that there is an 'inner smile' radiating from your pelvis – your hips, genitals and backside.

7. Now move to your legs and imagine that there is an 'inner smile' radiating from your legs – your thighs, knees and shins.

8. Move down to your feet and ankles and imagine that there is an 'inner smile' radiating from them.

9. Finally, consciously direct the energy of the 'inner smile' to your bones, blood, nervous system – to the whole of your body.

hormones, increases immune cells and infection-fighting antibodies, helps to release heavy emotions such as anxiety, anger or sadness, triggers the release of feel-good hormones, increases your sense of well-being, and helps you to shift perspective, allowing you to see situations in a new light. By the way, did you hear the one about the two caterpillars? Well, one day they are creeping through a wood when a butterfly passes by. One caterpillar turns to the other and says, 'Do you see that? Well, you will never catch me up in one of those!'

Who the hell wants to hear actors talk?

Harry Warner, Warner Brothers, 1927

Play and Creativity ...

Creativity is important in many professions, such as architecture, art, design, film, photography, television and writing, as well as business development, coaching, engineering, management, marketing, product development, training and teaching. Creativity is not something that is really taught in schools. As children, however, we are naturally creative and playful. As we forget to play we also forget to be creative.

One person who knew about creative play was Walt Disney. In his lifetime he won 26 Oscars for his films, the most ever given to an individual. He had an amazing ability to turn something that existed in his imagination into a form that gave people joy. Walt Disney had boundless energy, imagination and determination, but there was a secret to his success. When working on the early full-length cartoons that made his name, such as *Snow White*, *Pinocchio*, *Bambi* and *Fantasia*, he used a new creative approach to co-ordinate his film projects. He moved ideas for each film round three rooms – where each room had a different function. In the first room were placed the raw ideas. This was the room for dreaming; there were no limits or restrictions here; every outrageous hunch or idea was given the space to be developed. In Room Two, dreams from Room One were co-ordinated and a storyboard was created, allowing the storyline, characters and events to be fitted into sequence. (The idea of the storyboard was a Disney invention). In Room Three the whole crew would critically review the project. Here the project was pulled to pieces and criticized. Then the project was returned to Room One where work on the project would continue. The outcome was that either an idea did not survive Room Three and was abandoned, or it met with silence which meant it was ready for production.

Robert Dilts studied Walt Disney's creative process – writing about it in his book *Strategies of Genius: Volume 1*. Dilts helped to turn Disney's creativity strategy for making animated films into a strategy for success in any creative endeavour. Creativity can manifest in many different ways – through cooking, gardening or a business project. Creativity is about thinking, seeing things and acting in new ways. Robert Dilts realized that every creative project needed the three elements of creative imagination, practical action and critical refinement. Robert says about this, 'A dreamer without a realist cannot turn ideas into tangible expressions. A critic and a dreamer without a realist just become stuck in a perpetual conflict. A dreamer and a realist might create things, but they might not achieve a high degree of quality without a critic. The critic helps to evaluate and refined the products of creativity.'

EXERCISE

The Walt Disney Creativity Strategy

This exercise is best done in groups of three people. It is a process for playing with an idea, dream or creative project. Place three chairs in a triangle facing the centre. Choose who will be person A (the dreamer), person B (the realist) and person C (the critic), and sit down. Person A goes first. Persons B and C are the witnesses to the process. They are also the scribes that take notes and feed back at the end of each stage what has been said.

- **The Position of the Dreamer**. Person A speaks for five minutes about a dream or creative idea or project. Answer the question, 'What is the dream you most want to create?' Brainstorm all the possibilities – do not hold back, just explore this possible future.

- **The Position of the Realist**. Person B speaks for five minutes about the reality of creating this project. Answer the question, 'How are you going to create this dream?' Think about time frames, and how specifically will the idea be implemented? Who else needs to be involved and what resources do you need?

- **The Position of the Critic**. Person C speaks for five minutes about the pitfalls of this project. Look at how the elements do or do not fit together. Look at what is unnecessary and what is missing. Answer the question, 'Why should this project be re-thought or ditched?'

- **The Position of Reflection**. Go back to the position of the dreamer for a minute and, once again, ask yourself, 'Are you still willing to move forwards with this idea in light of what your realist and critic have said?' Then it's B and afterwards C's turn, until a final decision or plan has been reached.

Declaration of Intention

1. I am ready to witness and transform all suffering arising from my work. I am ready to release all limiting conditioning, beliefs, assumptions, unconscious agreements, obligations, drama, persecuting, rescuing and victim consciousness that appear to block me.

2. I am ready to be more authentic, present, conscious and aware in my life and work. I am ready to release any excessive reliance on living on autopilot. I am ready to be 100 per cent courageously myself.

3. I am ready to transform my attitude and perspective in my work. I am ready to face all my fears about the present and the future. I am ready to see a bright, expansive, inviting, hopeful future opening before me.

4. I am ready to acknowledge that my time on earth is limited. I am ready to acknowledge that my time is precious. I am ready to use my time more wisely.

5. I am ready to embrace the fullness of my gifts, resources, strengths and talents. I am ready to use my intellect with my imagination and intuition. I am ready to play to my strengths. I am ready to find my niche in the world. I am ready to listen to feedback and use it wisely.

6. I am ready for fun, humour, laughter and creative play in my work. I am ready to take myself lightly.

7. I am ready for fun, playful, supportive people to enter my life. I am ready to reach out and connect meaningfully with other explorers and pioneers in my chosen fields.

8. I am ready for my work to be a love affair. I am ready to know my heartfelt values. I am ready for enthusiasm and joy to enter into my work. I am ready to love the work I do. I am ready for my life's work to be revealed to me. I am ready to dream my work into being.

9. I am ready to flow like water rather than struggle. I am ready to take effortless action in alignment with my heartfelt values. I am ready to be in the right place at the right time. I am ready for my work to unfold with ease and grace. I am ready to work with ever more bliss.

10. I am ready to take this journey and find my own way. I am ready to trust in my inner guidance and see this journey through, wherever that shall lead me.

Chapter 10

Love Your Work

Work is love made visible. And if you cannot work with love but only with distaste, it is better that you should leave your work and sit at the gate of the temple and take alms of those who work with joy.

Kahlil Gibran

••

In the film *Pretty Woman*, Edward Lewis (played by Richard Gere), a successful and ruthless businessman, is driving along Hollywood Boulevard and stops to ask directions from a hooker called Vivienne (played by Julia Roberts). She offers to show him the way for a price. Edward agrees and she jumps in the car. Edward is intrigued by the vivacious Vivian and asks her up to his penthouse suite. The following morning he asks her to stay all week, and offers to pay her $3,000. During her stay Vivienne starts to have fun, and Edward gives her money for clothes. He spends an obscene amount of money on her and she is gradually transformed from a hooker to a lady.

Work as Love Affair ...

Most people do not love their work. It is possible to change your attitude to your work and start to enjoy what you do. It is also possible to change your work and start to do what your heart calls you to do. When the inner and the outer are in harmony, work is like a love affair. In ancient Greece there were different terms for love. There is love shared in a family such as the love a parent has for their child. There is the love found within friendship and close communities. Then there is a love so deep that you will sacrifice something of yourself for another. Then there is *Eros*, which is love in its passionate form. To the Greeks, this love was generally understood as a kind of madness – *theia mania* – from the gods.

Eros is a deep enthusiasm and joy. These feelings can arise within us through sensual work, such as working with wood, stone, clay and metal, or through photography and painting. It can come through massage or the performing arts. Nanne is an artist and I asked her about her work. She told me, 'I love getting up in the morning knowing that I am going to paint the whole day. Just to paint gives me energy, seeing the painting unfold before my eyes, every time the brush touches the canvas the painting is getting one step closer to the finished work. Being a painter, every step is a blessing for me, from the idea to the finished painting. I suppose I love to paint just to make people feel blessed.'

Eros can be with us whether we love painting or gardening, teaching or driving, sales or construction. Eros is about passion and desire. When we deny our desires we deny Eros entry into our work. *Washington Post* reporter Bob Woodward – who investigated the Watergate scandal – said, 'Getting up in the morning and having work you love is what makes life different for people. And if you get into a position where you really don't love what you're doing, get off it. It's easy to be on someone else's track or something that sounds like a safety play.'

Pilar was studying law in Spain and was in her third year. Then she took a holiday and in that space she realized that law was not her path. She felt her true passion was art, and so gave up law and studied a BA in Fine Art. Eros could not find her through law, she had no real passion for it. But through art Eros could flow.

Asta chose to study and pursue a career in finance, partly because her parents 'gently advised' her in this direction and partly because she did not really know what to choose. Every role she took in the 'corporate world' she found interesting, but she had no real sense of direction. She realized that she could work hard and achieve a certain degree of success, but deep down she had 'absolutely no desire to achieve that'! So she quit and did a number of random things such as volunteering, doing a certificate course in training, working in a retail shop during the Christmas season, and so on. These jobs gave her the space and confidence to discover things that really inspired her. It 'clicked' the night before her birthday when a Google search on the word 'philanthropy' led her to a Masters degree in Non-Governmental Organizations and Development. After completing her studies she found her dream job as an International Programmes Officer in an NGO that supports slum dweller communities in Africa and Asia to build housing and improve lives. I asked her why she loved this job and she said, 'I feel completely, absolutely at ease about where I am and feel no need to question whether I am in the right place. I know I am. I work with people that I look up to and want to be like. I get to travel and explore new places and cultures. My current role links all my strengths, skills and experiences, and interests. I feel like the job is the extension of the studies that I enjoyed – I am genuinely interested and curious about things related to my job. I am constantly learning something new. I have the privilege of meeting some of the poorest yet strongest and most resilient communities living on our planet. And my job reminds me to fully appreciate how blessed beyond any measure I am – we all are really – compared to the majority of the world's inhabitants.'

. . . .

Edward takes Vivienne to different social events to meet some of his associates. He also takes her on a date to the opera. Vivienne is moved by the music, and later that night they make love not as client and hooker but as lovers. The longer Edward spends with Vivienne, the more he is touched and transformed by his love for her. Slowly he changes from a ruthless businessman to a man with a heart and in the final scene we see Edward facing his fear of heights to climb up a fire escape with a rose in his mouth to woo his beloved Vivienne.

. . . .

Eros can flow through any form of work. The form of the work is not the important thing. It is whether you have a passion for that work or not. When you love what you are doing, Eros is flowing through you and touching those around you through your work.

Work as Love in Action …

It was in 2001 that I first visited the Findhorn Foundation in Scotland – founded by Peter and Eileen Caddy and Dorothy Maclean. I fell in love with the place and have been many times since. The Findhorn Foundation community has grown, since it was founded in the 1960s, into a living experiment in conscious living. The community includes an education centre, an arts centre, an ecovillage and over 30 different organizations and independent businesses. The community is based mainly at The Park, Findhorn and Cluny Hill College in the nearby town of Forres, but it also extends to individuals, businesses and organizations within a 50-mile radius. There are also satellite communities on the islands of Iona and Erraid on the west coast of Scotland.

The Findhorn community is based on a few core principles that encourage a deep inner listening and acting from that source of inner wisdom; co-creation with the intelligence of nature; work as being love in action; and service to uplift the world. The community holds a positive vision for the world and they pioneer, inspire, educate and encourage new ways of living and working together. On a daily basis people work together, meditate together, grow and prepare food together, build houses together, welcome guests together and sing, dance and celebrate together.

When I went there in the winter of 2001 it was a winter wonderland with snow and ice everywhere. I worked for a week in the vegetable garden and sometimes in the kitchen. Even though it was freezing, I loved working in the garden. There was such a spirit of camaraderie and common purpose. Before each period of work, people came together in a circle in silence and blessed the work that was about to be done. I had never, up until then, worked in this way before. In the kitchen there was also silence and blessing before any work was done. Also, after the meal was prepared there was a collective ritual of blessing that included the people about to enjoy the meal. This way of working was an eye-opening experience for me. And the good news is that you can experience this too, should you so wish. The Findhorn Foundation runs regular experience weeks where you can get away from your daily routine and experience conscious community and work as love in action. You can experience work as love in action and combine work with silence, laughter, blessing, friendship and a whole new way of being. If you have never experienced work as love in action before, then I highly recommend you try it out!

I am fortunate to work in an organization which is also based on the idea that work is love in action. Alternatives is a not-for-profit organization based in St James's Church, Piccadilly, London. For the past 30 years it has been promoting events with a diverse range of authors and teachers in the fields of spirituality and personal development. What I most love about Alternatives is that it is congruent with the hopeful message it seeks to promote in the world. One simple way we do this is to have a rule that the staff get out of the office twice a day to have tea together. This is a simple but effective way to check in, build friendship and connection, catch any issues before they become dramas, create space for creative solutions to challenges, and create space for creative ideas for new events or projects.

Another way we seek to work with the principle of love is work in action is to celebrate staff leaving and entering the organization. Towards the end of 2010 one of our directors decided to leave to pursue other interests. In the weeks leading up to her departure she received many emails from colleagues and people she had connected to through Alternatives, praising her contribution and wishing her well for the future. A few days before her leaving date we took her to dinner in an elegant restaurant and threw a party for her. She was deeply touched and tearful because of the 'wonderful' send off. Shortly after, we decided to recruit for two new posts in the organization and we interviewed several people. At the interviews we lit some candles and gentle incense and warmly welcomed each of the candidates. All of them were sincerely touched, saying afterwards that they had never had such a 'positive' interview experience before.

Eros and Values ...

We cannot talk about love at work without also talking about values. When we are working in alignment with our values we will love our work.

Diane is a mother of three children who is also a part-time complementary therapist. She works in a hospice giving reflexology and aromatherapy massage to cancer patients and motor neurone disease sufferers. I asked her what she most loves about her job and she replied, 'Talking to people and making them feel better about themselves.'

Janet loves bookkeeping and accounting. When I asked her what she most loved about her work she told me, 'The challenge of solving problems, fixing financial statements, finding missing income, making adjustments and then, voilá, the perfection when the financial statements are accurate. The beauty and challenges of organizing an accounting mess, taking piles of receipts, invoices and statements, organizing them, entering the data, and providing reports and financial statements in the end with everything organized and filed.'

Jeremy is a self-employed courier who drives around London delivering various parcels. I met him delivering a number of boxes to our office and I helped him carry them down. I was immediately drawn to his natural sense of joy and asked him whether he enjoyed his job. I was curious since I had met so many people doing this kind of work that seemed to resent what they were doing. He replied that 30 years ago he qualified as a lawyer and after getting his articles he realized that he was not suited for an indoor job. So he took a number of jobs, and eventually started a property business that gave him the money to travel. He travelled the world in a camper van, lived in Canada for a while and was now enjoying the outdoor life of a delivery man.

Amanda's career background is in real estate, advertising and retail sales. She also gained extensive personal experience in the medical/health profession as a caretaker for her husband. Following his death she wanted to dedicate her life to a higher cause. She moved from the UK to West Africa to work with repatriated refugees. Amanda values social justice and equality.

Sue loves working with young people. She says, 'They are rebels and full of energy most of the time and I love to challenge and encourage them. I tell them that they do not need to accept the status quo, I teach them people boundaries, because that is what they need most, after love and acceptance. I also teach them to try and fail, which is the best way to learn.' Sue is moved by her love to teach, inspire and change lives.

Debra loves event management and works with presenters who speak on personal and spiritual development. I asked her what she loved about her work and she replied, 'I love organizing and promoting events, meeting new people and getting positive feedback from people who have attended. I love to help people and this is a way I can make a difference in the world.' Debra is moved by her value for inspiration, learning, community and spirituality.

Michael has a passion for sales. When I asked him about his passion he told me, 'I wanted to be an entrepreneur and so I found the most entrepreneurial company I could find to provide me with sales experience and mentorship. I love serving and connecting with people. To me, when sales are done properly, it's like a great symphony orchestra playing in tune, perfectly timing each pitch, creating a beautiful masterpiece that brings both parties to a place of gratitude.' Michael values business, connection and integrity.

Eros and Inspiration …

A sense of values is one of the doors through which Eros can enter and enliven you. Another door is that of inspiration. Throughout history, creative people have used their imagination to dream up new possibilities. Early on, someone had the inspiration of using a flintstone to start a fire. Later, someone was inspired to invent the bow and arrow to hunt game. And someone was inspired to build a wheel and create horse-drawn transport. Through the ages, inspiration has helped to create civilization. Every great building, piece of art or music, and every great invention, was first just an inspiration in the creative imagination. In our modern world people are inspired to create all kinds of things. The internet was just an idea that later became a reality. Some of these inspirations have changed the course of history, such as the printing press, and others have become household items. For instance, at some point someone was inspired to invent mascara and teabags!

Eros enters us when we open to inspiration and we do this by opening our creative channel. The creative channel is opened when we get intensely curious about life, when we go out and look for what is amazing or joyful or inspiring around us. It is opened when we practise day-dreaming, when we expand our creative imagination and visualize things that could be. It is opened when we learn to improvise, try things out, and improve upon the ideas of others. You may have noticed how you tend to have a greater sense of aliveness when you think about dreams or creative solutions. Thinking about problems closes the door to Eros. You will certainly notice this quite quickly in your physiology – if you think about problems for a few minutes your body will naturally feel tense and will start feeling bad. When this happens you can be sure that Eros is leaving.

Eros is sensual and loves to touch you through the senses. He can touch you through a powerful film, evocative music, a gorgeous candlelit meal, or through the touch of the elements. Your imagination can open to the feel of bark, the warmth of the sun, the freshness of the sea or the coolness of a

EXERCISE 1

Open the Door to Eros

- Today start to notice colours that evoke a sense of joy in you.
- Read a book that ignites your imagination and passion.
- Watch a movie that touches and inspires you.
- Listen to music that brings you a sense of peace, beauty or love.
- Sit in a sunny place and enjoy the sensual experience of it.
- Touch different fabrics made from satin, wool, cotton, etc.
- Taste different things, then close your eyes and enjoy them even more.
- Go out and touch a tree, a rock, a leaf, a flower.
- Bathe or shower and just be aware of water.
- Explore your sense of smell with food, places, incense, essential oils, etc.
- Meditate on a colour or a sound.

breeze. A friend of mine, Edward, left university with a degree and 'nowhere to go'. He had no idea of what he wanted to do. He loved the outdoors and so he put together a flyer advertising gardening services through a couple of hundred letterboxes. He had never gardened before, but had read lots of books and thought, 'This can't be that hard.' Within a couple of months the business was going well and he was earning 'a good wage'! But he found gardening was a lonely business – then he remembered a dream he had as a kid of opening a café. Edward loved 'greasy spoons', Formica tables and most of all the ambiance of the traditional working man's café. He found a job in an American diner in Covent Garden, London, and started flipping burgers as a short-order chef. The work was fun and he was soon going out partying after work with his 'burger-flipping mates'. For the first time he had a job that

EXERCISE 2

Keep a Journal

One way to encourage your imagination is through journaling. Journaling can help you clarify your thoughts, needs and desires. Keep it with you at all times to jot down any ideas and thoughts related to your passions, goals, visions and dreams.

Here you can write about:

- What you think and imagine yourself doing; what interests and excites you;
- When you feel the most passionate;
- Conversations that inspire you;
- A book or film that moved you;
- A person or people you love being around;
- People that support you emotionally;
- A space that makes you feel creative or open or grateful;
- When you feel most in your flow.

he loved. Within several months he was managing that restaurant with aspirations of opening his own place. He found out how restaurants worked, and most importantly he found out how to cook. Three years later he realized his dream and opened a place in the Berwick Street fruit and vegetable market in Soho. Thirteen years later his café is still going strong and he still walks in and loves the work.

Eros and Enthusiasm ...

Joseph Campbell was a life-long student and teacher of the human spirit and mythology – not just the mythology of cultures long dead, but of living myth. Living myth makes itself known through anyone who has searched themselves and found their burning passion. Passion seeks fulfilment in the world. Joseph Campbell called the process of engaging passion in the world 'following your bliss'. This idea of following your bliss is not just about doing what you like, it is a matter of knowing your passion – what enthuses you – whether that be for business, coaching, dance, engineering, sports, travel or writing, and then just surrendering yourself to it. Of course, following your bliss can be challenging.

One person who followed his bliss and true calling is Matthew Fox. Matthew felt called to the priesthood and entered the Dominican order of the Roman Catholic Church. In the Church he obtained masters degrees in philosophy and theology and a PhD in spirituality. In following his bliss he became arguably the most important and controversial theologian of our time. This was not an easy path, since over time he developed ideas that challenged the heart of official Catholic doctrine. Among Matthew's most controversial teachings was a belief in 'original blessing', which became the title of one of his most popular books. This concept went directly against the core Church belief that we are all born into 'original sin'. He argued that there was a fourth element missing from the Christian Trinity – namely the

Mother, the feminine, which is the body, instinct, matter and nature. Also, his attitude of equality and compassion and social justice towards homosexuality brought him into conflict with the Church authorities. Not surprisingly, he was eventually asked to leave the Dominican order for 'disobedience'. To date, Matthew Fox has become an important figure in Creation Spirituality, and his book *The Reinvention of Work* has been pivotal in the defining of that movement. After hearing Matthew give a lecture on *The Reinvention of Work* I came away wishing that there were more passionate and visionary people like him preaching in the Church. I was in no doubt that if there were I would probably still be a practising Christian! Matthew asserts that life and livelihood are about spirit and he argues that that all work should have dignity. Most importantly, Matthew envisions a world of work in which the intellect, heart and body work together in celebration.

There is always challenge in following our bliss, but this is the way to feeling both materially successful and emotionally fulfilled. In his book *The Millionaire Mind*, Thomas Stanley researched the psychology of being a millionaire. He questioned over 700 millionaires on their attitudes, beliefs and lifestyles. He found that a common belief held by this group was that the way to sustainable wealth and an enjoyable life was through having a passion for the work they did. This group felt the more they loved their work, the more they were likely to excel and the more rewards they were likely to attract. Regardless of where you are in life, the first thing you need to do is realize that it's never too late to follow what you love. The next thing you need to realize is that you need to find it for yourself. The answer is inside of you and you will know it when Eros touches you.

Another person may think they know what you should do with your life, but if you feel nothing when you think about that possibility, Eros is saying it is not true for you. Just as with intuition, Eros speaks to you in the language of aliveness. Eros will speak through this channel often if you invite and allow him to. Eros speaks directly to each person. No two people will respond in the same way. No one else knows what makes your heart leap. The other thing to know about Eros is that he can be with you for a time and then he may leave. Perhaps a project or job sparks a tremendous sense of aliveness and then after a period of time it no longer does. Eros has left, and no matter how much you reinvent the role Eros will not return. This is a clear sign that you need to move on. Perhaps Eros is calling you to find new work that is more meaningful or fulfilling. Perhaps Eros wants to call you back to school, to start a business or to move somewhere new.

Raphaelle worked in a highly pressurized office-based job in overseas development. This was a career she had a certain amount of passion for and achieved some degree of success. But deep down there was something missing – her work was not really much fun, and it did not satisfy her creative

YOU KNOW WHEN EROS IS TOUCHING YOU WHEN ...

- You feel fully alive, energized and in your body.
- You feel fully in the moment.
- Your feel like you are resonating at a higher frequency than normal.
- You see things more clearly as if a veil has been lifted.
- You can talk about the things you love for hours.
- You feel that time ceases to exist.
- You find yourself at a new level of creativity.
- You start to think, feel and act in a new way.
- You feel that unseen hands are guiding you.

and artistic side. She told me, 'It was a difficult decision to leave a career that I had worked very hard for, that had earned me respect, a good salary and intellectual satisfaction. At first, I was at a loss as to exactly how I could earn a living doing what I truly loved. An interesting and difficult period followed. I sold my house, took some part-time jobs which I often found boring and frustrating – although not always, sometimes I got lucky! I had the time to put more energy into developing myself creatively. I took up piano lessons again – which I hadn't played since I had graduated. Somehow my next step became obvious in this period. Now, I have a small but successful piano teaching business. In the end, the most important factor in my decision was to take action on my own heart's longing. Essentially, I have more time … for a home life, for an artistic life and for a spiritual life. How wonderful is that!'

Eros and Dreaming …

Picasso once said, 'Dreams are like the paints of a great artist. Your dreams are your paints; the world is your canvas.' Dreams are the way we consciously shape our destiny.

The future is open; it is up to us to co-create it. When we train our conscious mind to focus on possibility rather than problems, almost anything is possible. There are many reasons why it is important to dream: a powerful dream gives a future focus away from the worries of the present and the past; a powerful dream creates positive psychological states; a powerful dream allows your imagination to soar; a powerful dream gives your life direction and guidance; a powerful dream helps to release your hidden gifts and talents; a powerful dream helps you stretch and grow towards a virgin future; and a powerful dream helps you to work in accordance with your values.

There is a big difference between dreaming and fantasizing. Dreamers are moving towards their visions, while fantasists are trying to escape from reality. Dreamers do not procrastinate, they do not lose focus, nor do they allow the opinions of others to distract them. Dreamers are concerned with the 'what' first and foremost. Thinking about the 'how' too early prevents the vision from taking shape. When the vision is big and compelling, the 'how' will take shape soon enough.

The Vision Board

To allow Eros in we must practise the art of dreaming. One very practical method to practise conscious dreaming is using something called the vision board technique. With this technique you do not have to visualize anything. A vision board is simply a visual representation or collage of the things that you want to have, be or do in your life. A vision board is a great way to get clear about your dreams and goals. It consists of a poster with cut-out pictures, drawings and/or words on it describing the things that you want in your life or the things that you want to become. Since your subconscious mind works in pictures and images, the vision board works very well. The imagery in this exercise conveys a clear set of instructions to your unconscious mind; the images are ones that generate a sense of happiness and passion within you to move forwards to your dreams and goals.

Woodrow Wilson once said, 'We grow great by dreams. All big men are dreamers. They see things in the soft haze of a spring day or in the red fire of a long winter's evening. Some of us let these great dreams die, but others nourish and protect them; nurse them through bad days till they bring them to the sunshine and light which comes always to those who sincerely hope that their dreams will come true.'

When we dream we are using our imagination to allow Eros to activate the resources of the unconscious mind, and these are vast. To give you an example of what I mean there is a true story about the well-known actor and comedian Jim Carrey. Early on in his career he was a struggling young comedian trying to make it in Hollywood. He was about ready to give up his dream of becoming a professional actor and comedian. He had just

Create a Vision Board

A vision board is a great way to get a little creative and more focused about what you want to create. You can prepare a vision board for your work, your relationships, or for a new project.

Materials. Basically, you need a board of some kind for the base, and a stack of different kinds of magazines that contain a variety of positive and colourful pictures and images. You will need a good photo of yourself, as well as some scissors and paper glue.

1. Sit in meditation and think about all the things you would love to attract or create in your life and work. Allow yourself to get silently enthused. Play with your imagination and with different mental images. Play with literal images such as you being offered a specific job in a specific company. Also play with metaphorical images such as a red rose for more love, a golden star for more success, a handful of jewels for abundance, a shimmering web in the sunlight for more heartfelt connections, and so on.

2. Go through the magazines and tear out the images that most fit your literal or metaphorical mental images of what you want to attract or create in your life. Create a pile of pictures.

3. Glue the picture of yourself in the middle of the board. Then start to create a collage of images around this central photo. Choose pictures from the pile that feel intuitively right and good.

4. When complete, hang your vision board in a place you will see it often. Perhaps by your bed so that your vision board is the last thing you see and think about before entering the sleep state and the first thing you will see when you open your eyes in the morning.

performed at an open mic session at one of the nightclubs in Los Angeles and had been booed off the stage by the audience. He sat by himself at the top of Mulholland Drive and looked out at the city below him – the city that held his future success or failure. He then pulled out his cheque book and wrote himself a cheque for $10 million dollars and made a note on it: 'For acting services rendered.' He then carried that cheque in his wallet everywhere he went from that day forwards.

Jim Carrey had activated the power of his unconscious mind. This is just one story of so many that I could tell you here. To activate the resources of your unconscious mind, start to think about your dream as if it has already happened. Start to consciously day-dream in pictures, sounds, feelings and words. This is a great habit to develop, since it will give clear instructions to your unconscious mind about where you want to head in life specifically. Anyone interested in performance and results will find this a useful technique to adopt. For instance, world-class athletes use this to achieve a great performance in their field. The best golfers visualize the shot before they hit the ball, and the best football players imagine scoring the goal before it happens. Actors use this method to rehearse in their minds what they want to experience. If you can imagine walking through the play and saying your lines and the play ending with rapturous applause, then you are creating a plan in your unconscious mind. This method is great when planning to give a great job interview. If you can imagine doing brilliantly in that interview, answering all the questions exactly as you would wish and then later being told that you have the job, then this will give you confidence. I have used this method very successfully with a number of coaching clients.

EXERCISE

Multi-Sensory Dreaming

State your dream – what you want to create or experience – in positive terms. Do not state it in terms of 'I do not want to create x', rather say, 'I want to create y'. Your unconscious mind does not understand a negative. Do not think of *a pink flamingo floating through the room now*, because by doing so your unconscious mind simply creates the image of *a pink flamingo floating through the room*.

1. Describe your positive outcome or dream in sensory-based language, meaning describe what you would see, hear, touch and smell when you experience this realized dream.

2. Imagine describing your dream in terms of the 'when', the 'where', the 'how' and 'with whom' you will create this dream outcome.

3. Imagine turning your dream outcome inside your imagination into a short video film. Imagine that you are in a cinema watching the film and yourself as an actor in this film. After a few minutes imagine stepping into the film and experiencing the dream as if it is happening around you.

THINK, REFLECT AND RESEARCH!

Think – about your achievements thus far, the skills and training you have picked up along the way, the resources you have developed. Also think about your ideal areas of work, your ideal work schedule, the minimum salary you need to live comfortably, your preferred commute time, the skills you would like to develop, whether you want to be employed, a freelancer, self-employed, or a mixture of these. Consider what needs to be in place to make work ideal for you? Do you want to take some time out?

Reflect – on your dreams, visions and values, your passions and heartfelt intentions. Ask yourself what inspires your imagination and what gives you the most joy in the world.

Research – read articles/books, attend seminars and networking groups, chat to friends, schmooze, ask for support or mentoring, take a career profiling test. When researching, also do something different and see how it feels.

Declaration of Intention

1. I am ready to witness and transform all suffering arising from my work. I am ready to release all limiting conditioning, beliefs, assumptions, unconscious agreements, obligations, drama, persecuting, rescuing and victim consciousness that appear to block me.

2. I am ready to be more authentic, present, conscious and aware in my life and work. I am ready to release any excessive reliance on living on autopilot. I am ready to be 100 per cent courageously myself.

3. I am ready to transform my attitude and perspective in my work. I am ready to face all my fears about the present and the future. I am ready to see a bright, expansive, inviting, hopeful future opening before me.

4. I am ready to acknowledge that my time on earth is limited. I am ready to acknowledge that my time is precious. I am ready to use my time more wisely.

5. I am ready to embrace the fullness of my gifts, resources, strengths and talents. I am ready to use my intellect with my imagination and intuition. I am ready to play to my strengths. I am ready to find my niche in the world. I am ready to listen to feedback and use it wisely.

6. I am ready for fun, humour, laughter and creative play in my work. I am ready to take myself lightly.

7. I am ready for fun, playful, supportive people to enter my life. I am ready to reach out and connect meaningfully with other explorers and pioneers in my chosen fields.

8. I am ready for my work to be a love affair. I am ready to know my heartfelt values. I am ready for enthusiasm and joy to enter into my work. I am ready to love the work I do. I am ready for my life's work to be revealed to me. I am ready to dream my work into being.

9. I am ready to flow like water rather than struggle. I am ready to take effortless action in alignment with my heartfelt values. I am ready to be in the right place at the right time. I am ready for my work to unfold with ease and grace. I am ready to work with ever more bliss.

10. I am ready to take this journey and find my own way. I am ready to trust in my inner guidance and see this journey through, wherever that shall lead me.

Chapter 11

Bliss at Work

What the caterpillar calls the end of the world,
the Master calls the butterfly.

Richard Bach

. . . .

It is said that when Prince Siddhartha sat under the Bodhi tree in meditation his mind was confronted with images of terrifying beings, some hurling spears, some firing arrows, some throwing huge boulders, and some showering him with fire. As he meditated the weapons and rocks became a shower of fragrant flowers, and the raging fires became fluttering rainbows. Then his mind was assailed by images of many beautiful women – he remained in meditation until all these delusions passed. Finally, when all these trials passed, he became awakened as the Buddha or 'Enlightened One'. His mind was clear and he was able to see deeply into the nature of reality. He saw how everything, from the smallest speck of dust to the brightest star, was interconnected in a constantly changing pattern. He saw that all things were impermanent, including what we consider the self. He also saw that all sentient life contained the potential for awakening. From this moment onwards the Buddha travelled for 45 years around the plain of the Ganges teaching the dharma of liberation, mindfulness, compassion and awakening.

THE FOUR POSSIBILITIES

1. There is the possibility that at some point in your work you will suffer, either physically, emotionally, mentally or even spiritually.

2. There is the possibility that you will transform your suffering and go beyond suffering and explore a new way, a more healthy and joyful way.

3. There is the possibility that you will know your true nature, become more resourceful, play instead of work hard, know your heartfelt values, follow your true direction, and find or create work that you love.

4. There is the possibility that you will learn to flow, take effortless action, open to grace and awaken to bliss in your work.

Our Potential for Bliss ...

Ananda was a close disciple of the Buddha. He was known as the Guardian of the Dharma ('dharma' meaning the teaching or way). The root of the name Ananda comes from a Sanskrit word meaning 'bliss', which is a state of deep happiness, joy and contentment.

Most images of the Buddha show him in a state of deep peace or joy. Bliss is living in the moment rather than in the imagined past or future. Bliss is living heaven on earth now. Beneath states of suffering exists the potential for bliss. Bliss has an inner and outer aspect. We can feel blissful for no reason. And we can feel blissful when engaging in something that creates in us a deep sense of joy such as meditation or work that we love. Spiritually speaking, bliss is an inner state that does not rely on any external conditions.

When the Buddha awakened he saw deeply into the nature of reality and saw that it contained three aspects. These have come to be known as the Dharma seals or marks. The first is that all life is impermanent and subject to forces of change. When we look out into the world we can see that nothing stays the same: the sun rises and then it sets, winter is followed by spring, children are born and then grow up, and buildings are constructed and in time crumble and fall. This is not something that is altered by belief. You may believe that you are immortal, but this does not insulate you from your mortality.

The second aspect the Buddha saw was that there is no fixed immutable self: what we think of as our personality or 'self' changes also. Again, this is not something that is altered by belief. It is certain that you thought and behaved differently at age 6 than at age 18. You think, feel and behave a certain way with your lover, and another way with your enemies. You will think, feel and behave a certain way when you feel on track in life, and another way when you feel aimless and drifting through life. We all change – there is no fixed unchangeable self.

The third aspect the Buddha saw was that everything contains the potential for liberation, awakening and bliss. This potential has come to be called Nirvana. The Buddha saw a vision of a pond full of lotus flowers. Some were still in the seed state in the mud at the bottom of the pond. Some had awakened and were rising through the water to the surface. And some were beautiful blossoms above the water. This blossoming is a state of 'luminous consciousness' that signals the end of suffering and the awakening of bliss. Tibetans refer to this as inner light or pure radiance. They say that this is a 'ground luminosity', since it is the bottom line of our being. There is nothing after this and nothing before this. Lama Surya Das says, 'This luminosity is birthless and deathless.'

It is worth noting that many Buddhists believe and teach the universality of suffering. In my view this is a mistake; suffering is not a universal aspect of reality, rather it is something generated by our attitude and habitual reactions to reality. Can we say that a flower suffers as it blooms under the sun? Can we say that a child suffers when being hugged lovingly by the mother? Can we say that an adult suffers when in nature watching a beautiful sunrise? On the other hand, can we say that a flower, a child and an adult all have the potential for awakening? A flower can awaken from the seed. A child can blossom with love. An adult can awaken in a moment of realization. The Buddha saw that all sentient beings have the potential for awakening into bliss. This is the teaching of the universality of awakening. Within you is a seed of awakening that can blossom through your work into a beautiful flower. This seed must be nurtured daily for it to awaken.

The Bliss of Action …

Action is the one thing that remains consistent throughout all the ages of work. Action is just as important to the hunter gatherer as it is to the knowledge worker. In the 1960s, towards the end of the Industrial Age, there was the idea of 'Turn on, tune in, drop out.' This was a time of spiritual awakening and also rebellion against the authoritarian style of the outgoing age of work. The current movement towards personal liberation is more like 'Turn on, tune in, step out.' Most spiritual pioneers have left behind the idea that we need to drop out from the world to find personal freedom. Of course, short retreats from the world can rejuvenate the spirit, but long-term retreat is not in the spirit of this emerging age.

Work involves action and engagement with the world. There is the day-to-day routine of action, and there is action that takes us beyond what we know. Day-to-day actions include getting up, brushing your teeth, eating breakfast, taking the kids to school, commuting to work, starting your work, having your morning tea break, and so on. Action that takes you beyond what you know includes taking time out, changing the way you behave and relate in your work, saying something that needed to be said for a long time, and taking a courageous step towards a new direction.

Action can be a means to liberation and new possibilities or it can lead us deeper into our habitual patterns and into suffering. For people with a pioneering mindset, work in the current Information-Virtual Age is an exciting place to be. It is easier now than ever before to put creative ideas into immediate action. Now it is possible very quickly to turn ideas into an online service or product. My own experience in this field is that although it is easy to make money via the internet through clever presentation and marketing, 'all that glistens is not gold'. There are those whose ethics do not prevent them from deceiving others. I once knew someone who was apparently interested in spirituality who had a website that was defrauding people. The product description in no way matched the product itself. He justified this by saying that he would always refund money when people complained. He was eventually persuaded that this was not an ethical way to make a living.

Actions that are in line with your values are more likely to lead to upliftment and joy. If you value learning and take actions to increase your understanding or develop a skill, then this will lead to joy. Actions that take you away from understanding or developing a skill will not lead to joy. If you value spirituality and you take actions to develop a spiritual practice, then this will lead to joy. Actions that take you away from developing a spiritual practice will not lead to joy.

Central to the Buddha's teaching on action was the concept of karma. Simply stated, the principle of karma is that actions have consequences and these follow a discernible pattern. These consequences are not only restricted to this lifetime. They can come to fruition in future lifetimes. Also, our actions have an impact on our nearest and dearest. Our descendants can benefit from actions based on love, courage and vision. One elderly man I knew had left school with few qualifications, but he had an entrepreneurial spirit within him and so created a successful import and export business. This business provided the funds to send his children to university. I met one of his sons who had followed his passion and trained to be a doctor and surgeon. When I met the son he was in his early 70s. He had very much loved his medical career and still worked on and off as a consultant. I also met his two children who were in their 40s. The son also trained as a doctor and had a great enthusiasm for his work. The daughter studied economics and went to work in publishing before following a new career in medical administration. She told me that her grandfather had been a great businessman and provider for the family. Apart from financing the education of his children and, in part, his grandchildren, he was also a great provider in other ways materially. They had enjoyed holidays because of his generosity and even gifts like pianos so they could play music at home. His entrepreneurial example had positively influenced his whole family. Now his great grandchild is a budding teenager who also seems to have the seed of a developing entrepreneurial spirit.

As you can see, our actions do not just impact ourselves, they cascade and touch those around us who we love. They will also ripple out and touch others that we hardly know. A smile or a kind word to a stranger can touch them so that they change how they go about their day. Perhaps, in turn, they will smile or say a kind word to a stranger and so the impact of the initial act of loving kindness ripples out into the collective. In Buddhist terms, actions can be skilful or unskilful rather than good or bad. Good intentions, though

• •

There is a story that the Buddha one day saw one of his followers meditating under a tree at the edge of the Ganges river. The Buddha stopped and inquired as to why he was meditating so intensely. His follower answered that he was attempting to become enlightened so he could cross the river unaided. The Buddha gave him a few coins and said, 'Why don't you seek passage with that boatman – it would be much easier.'

• •

THE FIVE PRECEPTS

The Buddha gave five principles or precepts to bear in mind when taking any action in the world.

1. Refrain from harming any living creature – rather practise loving compassion.

2. Refrain from taking that which is not given – rather practise generosity.

3. Refrain from sexual misconduct – rather practise kindness and respect.

4. Refrain from harmful speech – rather practise harmony and inclusivity.

5. Refrain from intoxicating drinks or drugs that lead to a dulling of the mind and senses – rather practise serenity and mindfulness.

important, are not enough by themselves. There is a saying that 'the road to hell is paved with good intentions'. A skilful action is that which is taken in a positive mental state. A positive intention coupled with intelligence, wisdom and appropriateness tends to lead to skilful actions. There are many degrees of positive mental states, such as being clear, inspired, enthused, loving, joyful or visionary. Unskilful action is that which is taken in a confused, angry or hateful state. Skilful actions tend to lead to fruitful and harmonious results. Unskilful actions tend to have poor-to-harmful results. Therefore, if you find yourself in a less than positive mental state it is better not to take action – unless confronted with real danger – rather, practise some of the exercises and meditations in this book to transform your mental state.

In our era the road to holiness necessarily passes through the world of action.

Dag Hammarskjold

The Bliss of Flow ...

Awakening to bliss has many elements, including the ability to flow in life. Mihaly Csikszentmihalyi, a psychology professor at the University of Chicago, studied people who know how to play entering a mental state he calls 'flow'. Csikszentmihalyi defines flow as 'the state in which people are so involved in an activity that nothing else seems to matter; the experience itself is so enjoyable that people will do it even at great cost, for the sheer sake of doing it.'

Csikszentmihalyi first became aware of flow when studying artists for his postgraduate thesis. As they worked, the artists seemed to go into a trance-like state. To his surprise he found that the finished product was less important to them than the process of doing the work itself. At first, he thought that this state would only occur in certain creative professions such as art or music. However, after thousands of interviews by his research team at the University of Chicago and other colleagues around the world, he found that flow was experienced by people from all walks of life across many different cultures.

What people did and why they did it varied immensely, but the quality of the enjoyment or flow produced was remarkably similar. In flow there is no clock watching, there is no awareness of time passing – the musician is one with the flow of music, the designer is one with the process of designing, and the manager is at one with the team. When we are in a state of flow our actions seem effortless and also more enjoyable and more rewarding. When we are in the right state of mind, then effortless action can follow.

The student who is in a state of heightened curiosity is more likely to learn than the student who is bored. The manager who believes and trusts in her staff is more likely to inspire great results than the manager who negatively judges the team.

EFFORTLESS ACTION – FLOWING LIKE WATER

You cannot make water flow uphill. Whenever you find yourself resisting or procrastinating, or forcing yourself to do something, just stop. Do something different, anything, until you start to feel more energy and engagement with what you are doing. This should lead to a sense of ease rather than struggle – water is meant to flow downhill.

Do not seek to push the river. When you are trying too hard to get somewhere, you are no longer flowing. Instead, slow down, relax and do less. Be in the moment and move with greater economy. Find ways of moving that produce greater results. Learn to allow events to unfold naturally. Suspend any plan or strategy and wait for the next step to become obvious.

Do not seek to control the river. When you seek to control others, or control your surroundings, you are no longer flowing. You are no longer in harmony with your surroundings. Instead, accept that you cannot control anything; be flexible and learn to flow around all obstacles with a minimum of effort.

Flow like water. Use your intuition and take effortless action, do not force anything; work cooperatively with others; where necessary work alone. Move away from activities that feel heavy towards activities that feel joyful and real.

Flow is being so absorbed in the activity that it becomes like a meditation. For instance, athletes recognize the Zone – a psychological space where mind and body work in perfect sync and movements seem to flow without conscious effort. The Zone is where performance improves dramatically. According to sport psychiatrist Dr Michael Larden, author of *Finding Your Zone*, 'The Zone is the ability to perform at your highest level in whatever domain of life you wish to enhance. It is not a phenomenon exclusive to sports; the Zone exists in all arenas, including business, art, music and sports. The secret to the Zone is that there is no secret. All of us possess the potential for accessing it.' When Roger Bannister broke the four-minute mile in 1954 he later said, 'No longer conscious of my movement I discovered a new unity with nature, I had found a new source of power and beauty, a source I never dreamt existed.'

Effortless action is a spiritual principle from Taoist philosophy that encourages pausing and resting from needless action and going with the flow. Effortless action is like flowing water – it can flow around obstacles to where it needs to go. Water never forces anything, it responds to the landscape and is gracefully powerful. Effortless action is about doing something, but it is not about strain, struggle or 'pushing the river'. Effortless action is knowing when to act and when not to act. It comes from having a vision and then paying attention to what needs doing. Effortless action happens when we get out of our own way. Just like playing a musical instrument. If you think about playing or try too hard to play, then you get in the way of your performance.

The Bliss of Synchronicity …

According to Frank Joseph, author of *Synchronicity and You*, 'Synchronicities are little miracles through which an otherwise Unseen Consciousness communicates with us. We may speak to the gods in prayer, but significant coincidence is the medium whereby they speak to us.' The term synchronicity was first defined by Carl Jung as two or more events that are apparently unrelated occurring together in a meaningful manner. Jung believed that life was not a series of random events, but rather an expression of a deeper order. One of his favourite quotes on synchronicity came from *Through the Looking-Glass* by Lewis Carroll. In this book the White Queen explains to Alice about the effects of living life backwards. 'Living backwards!' Alice says in great astonishment. 'I never heard of such a thing!' The Queen remarks, 'It's a poor sort of memory that only works backwards.'

Jung's concept of synchronicity was first inspired by a patient who had reached a certain impasse. Then one night, the patient dreamt of being given a golden scarab. When she was telling Jung about the dream, something knocked against the window pane behind Jung. Jung got up, opened the window and caught the insect. It was a golden scarab – a very rare occurrence for that climate.

Synchronicity transcends cause and effect and supposes a higher intelligence at work, one that moves through a fundamental unity of all things. Synchronicity can be unnerving – because it shows that we are not completely in control of our lives – or something to marvel at, depending on your point of view. Carolyn North, author of *Synchronicity: The Anatomy of Coincidence*, says about synchronicity that 'It gives us a sense of hope, a sense that something bigger is happening out there than what we can see.'

Synchronicity arises from intention; this is why each chapter ends with a Declaration of Intention. When you have a strong set of intentions, your unconscious mind knows what you want and can help to bring it to your attention. If you want more joy in your life and work, then at least with a strong intention for such your unconscious mind can grab your conscious attention and help you notice joy happening in and at the edges of your reality. When you have a powerful intention for creating more meaningful work – as long as you have a clear idea what that means to you – then your unconscious mind at least has something to go on to help you create that intention. One way the unconscious mind does this is through synchronicity. Synchronicity reminds us of our dreams and reveals a more meaningful direction for our lives – one that is not fully conscious.

My own journey of finding more meaningful work really began with a couple of synchronicity moments. I was an unhappy manager working for local government, thinking about whether to resign or not. I wanted more meaningful work. I was not completely sure about the form of the works, but I was sure that I wanted more creative work that gave me a greater sense of freedom and autonomy. I mentally asked the question to 'the Universe' and soon received a number of replies that gave an emphatic 'yes', saying 'just do it'. The Sufi poet Rumi once said that it is better to live the questions than always to know the answers. Living with questions rather than answers can feel confusing because it requires that we do not see up-front the whole design, only pieces of the puzzle. According to David Richio, author of *Unexpected Miracles*, 'Synchronicity is the surprise that something suddenly fits! Synchronous events are meaningful coincidences or correspondences that guide us, warn us, or confirm us on our path.'

Sometimes synchronicity leads us beyond our fears in pursuit of some higher dream. Margaret Munnerlyn Mitchell was asked by a friend to escort the editor of a publishing house, who was visiting Atlanta looking for promising writers in the South. The editor asked her if she had ever thought about writing a book. Margaret said 'no'. Later that day, a friend of Margaret's heard about the conversation and laughed. 'Imagine anyone as silly as her writing a book!' Margaret was so indignant over the comment that she went home and dug out a manuscript she had completed. She arrived at the editor's hotel just as he was preparing to leave and gave him the manuscript, saying, 'Here, take this before I change my mind!' In 1937 Margaret Munnerlyn Mitchell won the Pulitzer Prize for her novel *Gone with the Wind*, which is possibly one of the most popular books of all time, selling more than 30 million copies to date.

James wanted to train in coaching and NLP, but he did not have the money – the training he wanted to do cost between five and seven thousand pounds. Then, through some friends, he was introduced to Mike who ran an NLP training business. The two became friendly – and one day over tea Mike 'coincidentally' revealed that his operations manager had just handed in her notice and asked James if he knew anyone experienced and interested in such a job. James could not believe his ears – he just so happened to have some relevant experience in an events management company and asked Mike to try him out. 'Coincidentally', one of the perks of the job was that all the training came for free. James got the job and also his wish to train in coaching and NLP. He completed his training with flying colours – which he told me he absolutely loved – and he now runs his own private coaching practice.

Synchronicity can happen to us at any stage of life. I met Sarah at a Bahia gathering at a friend's house a few years back and asked what she did. She said that she was an actress and a singer. Intrigued, I asked her if she would sing for the guests and to my surprise she agreed. Suddenly, I was just blown away by the power and beauty of this young woman's voice. She stopped the party and the other guests quickly gathered around to see who had this amazing voice. Soon after, I thanked her and also asked her about how she got into theatre. She replied, 'I knew I wanted to be in the world of theatre from a young age. It started when I was just twelve, someone gave me a video of the making of the highly successful play *Miss Saigon*. I instantly fell in love with the lead part. Being part-Filipino and part-English I knew I had the right look, but just as importantly I had a strong sense of self-belief and trust. By the age of seventeen I landed a part in the London West End show and two years later I was singing the lead role of Kim in Sweden. Five years after that, I was playing the lead role of Princess Anjuli in the West End show *Far Pavilions*. These parts felt like they were almost dropped down from heaven for me.'

I walked to the pier today

Inspired by the golden rays

And suspended atop the watery womb

Breathing ocean mist and sunlight

I am suddenly awake.

Katie Gallanti

Awakening to Bliss …

Practically speaking, we are living through a time where work markets are very volatile – everything is changing at rapid speed. Your well-conceived plan may be out of date in a few months. This is why having a clear intention is better than having a fixed plan. With an intention there are many routes to achieve the end result. With a plan there is less flexibility and fewer options. Interestingly enough, I recently read that the CEO of Google said that Google have a clear mission but no plan. In view of their amazing creative and financial success I guess not having a plan is no bad thing!

We have previously explored the benefits of adopting a playful attitude at work. One of the greatest benefits of this is that it prepares us to live without needing to know what is just ahead. This is a real skill that is becoming increasingly important as work is becoming less predictable. No one knows what will happen in the next year or so, let alone the next decade. Often fulfilment, love and success come upon us despite our plans. Bliss is waiting for us beyond the edge of what we know. And this means giving up our plans or fixed ideas as to how things will turn out.

Sometimes the process of awakening to bliss happens through intention and perseverance. For instance, Beatrice struggled for some years in low-paid retail work. Then she decided to train to become a yoga teacher. Upon completion she worked as a teacher part time, and then her work grew and she taught on a more full-time basis. She felt more alive, she had more space and time in her life to focus on what she loved doing. Then she decided to follow her passion for spiritual counselling. She started to see clients and integrate this work alongside her yoga. For Beatrice, her journey into bliss was not a dramatic awakening, but a series of inspirational ideas coupled with taking small steps towards what she loved doing.

Sometimes an awakening into bliss happens suddenly and unexpectedly. I know a corporate coach and trainer who had a sudden and dramatic spiritual awakening experience at work. It happened unexpectedly after speaking with a business client on the phone – at the end of the call, for no reason he began crying and couldn't stop. This initially led to a difficult space where the feeling was so powerful he thought he was dying. This eventually passed and led to a beautiful state so intense that he 'continued to cry almost every day for the next year'. Because of the intensity of the experience he was not able to work for a while. Then, eventually, he did return to work, but this time with a very different state of consciousness – one of permanent presence, peace and bliss. His work has not changed, but he has changed forever.

Whether bliss happens gradually or suddenly it will happen in its own good time. We cannot force bliss. The good news is that it does not matter if you have suffered for years, bliss is always a possibility. I absolutely hated my first job with a passion and I stayed in this way of suffering for ten years. At the time I thought this was how my working life would always be. Now I realize that suffering can always change into something more enjoyable and useful.

The Bliss of Good Fortune …

Joseph Campbell says, 'Follow your bliss and the universe will open doors where there were only walls.' Divine providence is about the miracle of life – which is happening all around us all of the time. That this earth spins around a golden warming sun at just the right distance, not so close that we are burnt to a cinder and not so far away that we freeze, is a miracle. That the earth has a gravity that is not so strong that it crushes life and not so light that it allows life forms to float into outer space is also a miracle. There are many other miracles that we daily take for granted. That you have health, inner resources, and the ability to move and create in the world are also miracles. Saint Augustine said, 'Miracles are not contrary to nature, but only contrary to what we know about nature.'

We can choose to deny the miracle of life or we can accept the miracle of life and decide to do something meaningful with it. The late Steve Jobs – co-founder of Apple – was adopted as a baby. When he was still a child his adoptive parents moved to live in Santa Clara County, south of San Francisco, later to become known as Silicon Valley. So he grew up surrounded by the curious world of electronics. At school he met Steve Wozniak – who went on to co-found Apple with Jobs – and at school they started their first joint entrepreneurial venture, selling illegal phone devices to Berkeley students. Later at college, Jobs had no idea what he wanted to do with his life and no idea how college was going to help him, so he dropped out and took up a calligraphy class. This was really random since it seemed to have little practical application. Later, it was to have a profound impact on the design of the Apple computer. After college, Jobs took a job with Atari, a manufacturer of popular video games and home computers, with the primary aim of saving money for a retreat in India. Jobs then travelled to India with a friend – who later became the first Apple employee – in search of spiritual enlightenment. He came back a Buddhist with his head shaved. Interestingly, Jobs later considered becoming a Buddhist monk instead of starting Apple, but a spiritual guru convinced him otherwise. Apple revolutionized the world of personal computing – making Steve Jobs a billionaire – and it all happened without any overall plan. There was just a unifying sense of passion that strung together a thread of meaningful coincidences. Steve said about these times in his life, 'You can't connect the dots looking forward; you can only connect them looking backwards. So you have to trust that the dots will somehow connect in your future. You have to trust in something – your gut, destiny, life, karma, whatever. This approach has never let me down, and it has made all the difference in my life.'

Shirlie started out in rock music in the 1970s working with Ray Davies and the Kinks, and other bands such as Ultravox, Hot Chocolate and Suzie Quatro – by the 1980s she was writing and performing for musical theatre. She was involved in the performances of hit shows such as *Fiddler on the Roof* and *Joseph and the Amazing Technicolor Dreamcoat*. After her own rock opera at Sadler's Wells was panned by the critics she hit a kind of 'dark night of the soul'. She came out the other side and decided to change her life completely and sent out a prayer to spirit, saying, 'I will go wherever you ask me to go, I will do whatever you ask me to do, I will be with whomsoever you ask me to be with, in service to the planet and the people.' Shortly afterwards, 'the doors swung wide open in the newly-formed Republic of Slovenia', where she has been doing concerts since 1992 and also healing sound seminars and workshops – she teaches the use of the voice as a healing instrument. She is affectionately known as the Ambassador of Light in Slovenia. Working in Slovenia opened doors for work in other countries, including Egypt where she is now leading sound retreats. Shirlie says about her work, 'Singing brings us all alive. It connects us – not only to each other, but to the vibration of the whole universe.'

In October 2010, I met Jeni on a training course I was running in Sofia. She was my translator and she was really great to work with. She came on the seminar with two important dreams. The first was to complete a teacher training course and the second was to find work that would enable her to live in the Middle East and travel. The challenge for the first was that she did not have the money to do the course. The challenge for the second was that she wanted to work as an air hostess, but had already recently failed the initial screening and height test with the airline of her choice. After the seminar she was having tea with a participant and she shared her first dream. To her complete surprise – she nearly fell off her chair – he had come into some money recently and offered to pay for her teaching course. After a month, she reapplied for the airline and this time got accepted! Although a little nervous, she passed both the interview and height test with flying colours – bearing in mind that presumably one cannot change their height so quickly. Jeni said about this, 'The height thing was even more extraordinary than being given the money because I thought I have no way to change my height.' Well, strange things happen I guess – anyway it was so wonderful to hear that her dreams had been realized in such a short time, with only a little change of attitude.

INVITE GOOD FORTUNE INTO YOUR WORK

- Know your intentions and let go of any attachment to results.
- Intend for grace, divine providence and bliss to show up in your work.
- Let go of your need to do it all by yourself.
- Trust that the Universe is friendly and intelligent and is working on your behalf.
- Start to believe that grace can happen to you at any time.
- Open to good fortune entering your life in different unexpected ways.
- Be thankful when grace and good fortune arrive.
- Take action in the faith that the best outcomes are unfolding in your life and work.

Declaration of Intention

1. I am ready to witness and transform all suffering arising from my work. I am ready to release all limiting conditioning, beliefs, assumptions, unconscious agreements, obligations, drama, persecuting, rescuing and victim consciousness that appear to block me.

2. I am ready to be more authentic, present, conscious and aware in my life and work. I am ready to release any excessive reliance on living on autopilot. I am ready to be 100 per cent courageously myself.

3. I am ready to transform my attitude and perspective in my work. I am ready to face all my fears about the present and the future. I am ready to see a bright, expansive, inviting, hopeful future opening before me.

4. I am ready to acknowledge that my time on earth is limited. I am ready to acknowledge that my time is precious. I am ready to use my time more wisely.

5. I am ready to embrace the fullness of my gifts, resources, strengths and talents. I am ready to use my intellect with my imagination and intuition. I am ready to play to my strengths. I am ready to find my niche in the world. I am ready to listen to feedback and use it wisely.

6. I am ready for fun, humour, laughter and creative play in my work. I am ready to take myself lightly.

7. I am ready for fun, playful, supportive people to enter my life. I am ready to reach out and connect meaningfully with other explorers and pioneers in my chosen fields.

8. I am ready for my work to be a love affair. I am ready to know my heartfelt values. I am ready for enthusiasm and joy to enter into my work. I am ready to love the work I do. I am ready for my life's work to be revealed to me. I am ready to dream my work into being.

9. I am ready to flow like water rather than struggle. I am ready to take effortless action in alignment with my heartfelt values. I am ready to be in the right place at the right time. I am ready for my work to unfold with ease and grace. I am ready to work with ever more bliss.

10. I am ready to take this journey and find my own way. I am ready to trust in my inner guidance and see this journey through, wherever that shall lead me.

The Bliss of Truth …

From the wisdom of Huna – from Hawaii – comes a very useful principle that says 'Effectiveness is the measure of truth.' This principle – called Pono – states that there is always another way to do anything. We never have to be stuck in one method or way. There is no one truth, no one method, no one technique, no one philosophy, and no one way to be happy and successful. Even though your sense of passion and purpose is sacred, your means to achieving that purpose is not. This does not mean doing anything against your values or ethics – far from it, rather it says always try another way. Just as in chess there are many ways to move throughout the game. No one – and no computer – has figured all the variations.

Do not treat any of the ideas in this book or any other as the only way. Remain unattached. There are many ways, many permutations to move towards work that will awaken and fulfil your heart. You have your own path, discover it! Only take those ideas that feel useful and practical. It is my wish that this book will help you find the inner strength to be bold, intuitive, innovative and flexible in your approach.

And so there we have it – as we know, all things are impermanent! I am so grateful to have shared this part of the journey with you. And your journey continues onwards beyond these pages. I want to take this opportunity to bless your journey of work. May you know the true work of your heart and as a result awaken to flow, play, passion and bliss. When your work is the true work of your heart, then it becomes a real contribution to yourself, your family, your intimate community, your descendants, and the world at large.

With love and blessing

Steve Ahnael Nobel

．．．

The Buddha encouraged his disciples not to waste their time and energy in metaphysical speculation. Whenever he was asked a metaphysical question he would remain silent. Instead, he directed his disciples towards practical efforts. One day he said, 'Suppose a man is struck by a poisoned arrow and the healer wishes to take out the arrow immediately. Suppose the man does not want the arrow removed until he knows who shot it, his age, his parents, and why he shot it. What would happen? If he were to wait until all these questions have been answered, the man might die first.' Life is short, do not waste time in metaphysical speculation that does not bring you any closer to the truth.

．．．

Resources

Recommended Books on Work

Boldt, Laurence, *How to Find the Work You Love,* Arcana, *1996*

Bolles, Richard, *What Colour is Your Parachute?*, Ten Speed Press, 1998

Covey, Stephen, *The Seven Habits of Highly Effective People*, Simon & Schuster, 2004

Ferris, Timothy, *The 4-Hour Workweek*, Crown Business, 2007

Fox, Matthew, *Reinvention of Work,* Harper San Francisco, 1995

Holden, Robert, *Success Intelligence*, Hay House, 2010

Moore, Thomas, *A Life at Work,* Three Rivers Press, 2009

Pink, Daniel, *A Whole New Mind*, Marshall Cavendish, 2008

Whyte, David, *Crossing the Unknown Sea,* Penguin Books, 2001

Williams, Nick, *The Work We Were Born To Do*, Element Books, 2000

Recommended Books on Buddhism

Chodron, Pema, *The Wisdom of No Escape*, Element, 2004

The Dalai Lama, *The Art of Happiness*, Mobius, 1999

Kabat Zinn, Jon, *Coming to Our Senses*, Piatkus, 2005

Kornfield, Jack, *After the Ecstasy, the Laundry*, Rider, 2000

Lama Surya Das, *Awakening the Buddha Within*, Bantam, 1997

Thich Nhat Hanh, *The Heart of Buddha's Teaching*, Rider, 1999

Recommended UK Buddhist Websites

The Buddhist Society – www.thebuddhistsociety.org

Gaia House – www.gaiahouse.co.uk

Jamyang – www.jamyang.co.uk

Kagyu Samye Dzong – www.london.samye.org

Mindfulness London – www.learnmindfulness.co.uk

Samye Ling – www.samyeling.org

Triatna (previously Friends of the Western Buddhist Order) –
   www.fwbo.org

Recommended International Buddhist Websites

Pema Chodron, USA – www.pemachodronfoundation.org

The Dalai Lama, Northern India – www.dalailama.com

Dharma Seed, USA – www.dharmaseed.org

Heart of Asia – www.heartofasia.org

Jack Kornfield, USA – www.jackkornfield.org

Lama Surya Das, USA – www.surya.org

Plum Village, Southern France – www.plumvillage.org

Shambhala International, worldwide – www.shambhala.org

Ed and Debs Shapiro, USA – www.edanddebshapiro.com

Spirit Rock, CA. USA – www.spiritrock.org

Vipassana Meditation, worldwide – www.dhamma.org

Recommended Campaign Websites

Burma Campaign – www.burmacampaign.org.uk

Free Tibet – www.freetibet.org

Heart of Asia – www.heartofasia.org

Karuna, India – www.appeals.karuna.org

Tibet Foundation – www.tibet-foundation.org

Tibet Society – www.tibetsociety.com

Contacting the Author

The author's main site – www.stevenobel.com – includes information on seminars in the UK and Europe, and 1-to-1 coaching.

FREE Podcasts – www.stevenobel-audio.com provides various audio on different subjects by the author, including the theme of enlightened work, and www.stevenobel-interviews.com again provides lots of audio – this time the author is interviewing other authors and teachers on a broad range of subjects.

Alternatives, St James's Church, Piccadilly, London – www.alternatives. org.uk – is a not-for-profit organization that promotes authors and teachers in the mind, body, spirit fields – the author is a co-director.

Facebook – the author has a Facebook fan page: search for *Steve Ahnael Nobel*

Twitter – Find the author under *London_Has_Soul*

Contact email – you can contact the author via lotus-sword@gmx.com

Index